THE FLIRTING BIBLE

Text © 2010 Fran Greene
Photography © 2010 Rockport Publishers

First published in the USA in 2010 by
Fair Winds Press, a member of
Quayside Publishing Group
100 Cummings Center
Suite 406-L
Beverly, MA 01915-6101
www.fairwindspress.com

14 13 12 11 10   1 2 3 4 5

ISBN-13: 978-1-59233-421-6
ISBN-10: 1-59233-421-0

Library of Congress Cataloging-in-Publication Data
Greene, Fran.
  The flirting bible : your ultimate photo guide to reading body
language, getting noticed, and meeting more people than you ever thought
possible / Fran Greene.
     p. cm.
  ISBN-13: 978-1-59233-421-6
  ISBN-10: 1-59233-421-0
  1. Flirting. 2. Interpersonal communication. 3. Interpersonal
attraction. 4. Man-woman relationships. I. Title.
  HQ801.G6838 2010
  306.73–dc22
                    2010008992

Cover design by DoubleMRanch.com
Book design by Traffic Design Consultants Ltd.
Book layout by Megan Jones Design
Photography by Luidi Hara Photography

Printed and bound in China

THE FLIRTING BIBLE

Your **ULTIMATE PHOTO GUIDE** to Reading Body Language, Getting Noticed, and Meeting More People Than You Ever Thought Possible

FRAN GREENE

Former Director of
Flirting at Match.com

FAIR WINDS
PRESS
BEVERLY, MASSACHUSETTS

TO MY MOTHER, ROZZIE GREENE, WHO WAS THE MOST FABULOUS FLIRT.
THANKS FOR GIVING ME THE "FLIRTING" GENE. I LOVE YOU.

AND TO MY TERRIFIC HUSBAND, DR. JAMES MULLIN, ALSO KNOWN AS "EXHIBIT A."
I LOVE YOU MORE TODAY THAN YESTERDAY AND LESS THAN TOMORROW.

CONTENTS

PART ONE

Your Move-by-Move Guide to the **BODY LANGUAGE** of Flirting

INTRODUCTION
BE A NATURAL FLIRT IN NO TIME!

My own flirting story is the inspiration for this book and the reason I met the love of my life. It happened to me, and it can so easily happen to you. And it's proof positive that flirting can spark love.

I have always been an outgoing person, but during my twenties, I made "putting myself out there" my full-time job. Determined to find a husband, I did everything in my power to make it happen: blind dates, singles events, bar outings, personal ad placements, cruises, parties—you name it. I flirted anywhere and everywhere and made each event an exciting journey. Several adventures led to dates, others to boyfriends, some to great one-time meetings, and many to no-thank-yous. A few even led to broken hearts. Still, I never regretted trying.

As a full-time flirt, I rarely waited for someone to approach me. It just seemed such a waste of precious time. Going to a singles bar or event alone motivated me to flirt. If I didn't, the evening would be painfully boring, frustrating, and disappointing. (I know many of you are thinking, "No way, not me! Going somewhere alone is too scary and overwhelming." Rest assured, in the pages to come, I will help you through this process. Eventually, you may even look forward to solo-sailing! Trust me.)

Whether alone or with friends, I flirted no matter where I went: dining out, attending a concert, waiting in line, getting gas, talking to the letter carrier, even sitting in class—location never mattered. I was always "on the flirt." To me, flirting made every situation more enjoyable and fun, made me feel good and others feel great, and increased the chances of my dream coming true.

Like anyone, I felt the occasional frustration or discouragement looking for love. But I never gave up (though I did let go of the myth that love just happens). I knew that anything important in life takes work. I must admit, I was envious of those who said that love just found them—lucky them! But I persevered.

One day, after a lengthy meeting, I went to lunch with a group of colleagues. There were eight of us, seven women and one man. Jim worked at a sister office so I had met him for the first time earlier that day. He was nice and good-looking, so I decided to sit next to him at lunch to try out some of the flirting moves I had picked up and perfected from my "flirting fieldwork." I was complimentary, funny, leaned in when he talked, smiled, maintained warm eye contact, listened attentively, and showed interest. Over lunch, we had a great time getting to know each other, but we left it at that.

Fast forward three months. Jim came to our office for another meeting. After it ended, I offered him a ride to the airport. He said yes but on the condition that I went to dinner with him beforehand. I agreed (of course!).

As we left for the restaurant, we passed the office of a woman who knew I was not married. She jokingly yelled out, "Fran, is that your new husband?" Jim put his arm on my shoulder and replied, "I should be so lucky!" His words made me smile from ear to ear, and I quickly whispered back, "No, I should be so lucky."

Three years later, we were married.

My story is not unique. During the past twenty years, I have taught how-to-flirt workshops to thousands of single, divorced, and widowed men and women and have watched many of them find love. It is truly an amazing thing. This book has grown out of their personal struggles with how and where to meet new people, as well as their successes. (If my success rate is any indication, you may well find the love of your life by following my lessons!)

As I have taught them, I will teach you. I will show you how to master the art of flirting and reading body language—and I promise you'll have fun doing it! But just as I am committed to giving you a step-by-step guide that will better enable you to find love and excitement, you will have to be ready, willing, and able to flirt like a pro—or at least try! If you do, you'll experience limitless rewards.

Flirting works! Now let's get started.

Forever your flirt,

Fran Greene

CHAPTER ONE
THE SECRETS OF FABULOUS FLIRTING

OUR DESIRE TO FIND SOMEONE WITH WHOM TO SHARE OUR LIVES bonds all of us together. Yet often, we approach this task passively and haphazardly, leaving it to fate or chance. Many of us spend years wishing and hoping for the loves of our lives to come knocking. Wouldn't it be great if you could snap your fingers and s/he would arrive on the scene?

I, too, wish that could be true, but consider the following: Anything really important in life takes time, work, perseverance, and resilience. For most of us, finding love is a process. Flirting makes that journey fun, exciting, and challenging.

What is flirting exactly? It's a series of nonverbal and verbal actions we do when expressing our interest in or attraction to another person. Flirting is playful, nonthreatening, and sometimes subconscious. It's about displaying and reading body language.

Know how to flirt, and you can meet people ordinarily too terrifying to approach. Through flirting, you get to express yourself in inventive and ingenious ways, create a stimulating environment, and set the stage for romantic interest. Not only is it exhilarating for the flirter, but it's also a real ego boost for the flirtee. When you flirt, you feel energized and confident—feelings that become your love building blocks, the foundation for your journey.

Where may your journey take you? It can take you anywhere! A flirtatious encounter could, for example, lead to a shared interest, friendship, professional connection, romance, relationship, marriage, or one-time encounter you will remember forever. No matter the outcome, a sense of magic surrounds flirtation.

Though flirting can be splendid, it can also be downright scary! Let's start by addressing our fears and working past them. I guarantee it will be worth it.

DIMINISH YOUR FLIRTING FEAR

Do you ever get sweaty palms, dry mouth, a pit in your stomach, or anxiety before you approach a cute guy or gal at a party? Do you obsess over questions such as these:

- Should I walk over?
- What should I say? What should I *not* say?
- Should I try to make eye contact?
- Will s/he blow me off?
- What if I don't end up liking him/her?
- What if s/he doesn't like me?

Fear can be debilitating. It prevents you from taking risks that could help you attain what you want. Remember, we are all afraid. When I ask workshop participants to raise their hands if they fear rejection, typically about 99 percent of students do.

FLIRTING TIP: TURN YOUR FAUX-PAS INTO COMEDY

Did you inadvertently do something silly or embarrassing? Turn the situation into something fun and playful. Your self-assuredness will surely impress.

Let's say, for example, you come out of the ladies room and notice a piece of toilet paper stuck to your shoe. At the same moment, Mr. Wonderful walks by and says hi. What do you do?

Ask Mr. Wonderful to borrow his foot. No one has ever asked him that before, he replies, but he agrees. You then ask him to step on the paper to unstick it from your shoe. Offer to repay him with a drink.

If you are one of these individuals—and trust me, we all are—take a deep breath and tell yourself the following:

- If I do nothing, I get nothing.
- Trying will make me feel good. I took a risk.
- S/He could be the one for me.
- Even if s/he is not interested, I will be able to exit gracefully.

Remembering these axioms will reduce your anxiety and increase your opportunity for success. If the person you approach doesn't reciprocate your flirtatious gesture, you will depart subtly. This will be easy because your approach was light and nonthreatening (we'll get into how to do this in later chapters).

Flirting is a sensational way to connect with someone, and it allows you to be playful and casual without a heavy come-on.

FROM THE FLIRTING FIELD

Renee, twenty-five, and Heidi, twenty-six, two former workshop attendees, were at a singles bar when they spotted two guys they wanted to meet. Though they weren't sure what exactly to say or do, they remembered that being fun and playful could take them far. Renee grabbed Heidi, walked over to the guys, and said, "We just took a how-to-flirt workshop and our assignment was to approach two nice, attractive guys..."

Sean and Marc, both twenty-eight, were flattered, and the four of them talked for an hour. Sean asked for Heidi's phone number, and Mark wanted to fix up Renee with his friend. You just never know where flirting may lead.

IF I DON'T FLIRT, THEN WHAT?

You will miss many opportunities if you stick to the sideline, waiting for *it* to happen. *It* doesn't happen on its own. You have to go after it.

What is *it*? It could be the man or woman of your dreams, the highlight of your day, a new business contact, or the knowledge that the best sushi in town is down the block. Whatever *it* is, it can't happen if roadblocks—excuses you cling to for fear of stepping outside of your comfort zone—get in your way.

Look at the following chart. The first column lists potential flirting roadblocks that put you in a safe, cozy, comfortable zone. It feels good to be there, right? But it's not, really. These

FROM THE SIDELINES TO THE FLIRTING FAST LANE

Ice-cold Pessimism	Red-hot Optimism
Safe is better than sorry.	Taking a risk brings me great things.
I should avoid talking to strangers.	A stranger today may be a wife or husband tomorrow.
If I wait long enough, good things will happen.	Make good things happen.
Women who approach men are needy.	Women who approach men are confident.
Men who approach women only want one thing.	Men who approach women *do* want one thing—to make a meaningful connection.
Singles events are the only places to flirt.	Fabulous flirts flirt everywhere.
It's a waste of time to attend a party where I know only the host.	Parties full of people I don't know are my flirting paradise.
Dining alone screams "loser."	Dining alone is a great way to meet someone.
I shouldn't talk to someone I don't know until I am introduced.	The quicker I introduce myself, the more fun I will have.

myths give you false security because they steer you away from what you want. They keep you stuck in a flirting rut. The red-hot statements, on the other hand, put you on a surefire path to flirting success. They keep your mind and heart open to any situation.

Roadblock Statement: "Safe Is Better Than Sorry"

When it comes to walking on wet floors, looking both ways before you cross the street, or washing your hands, sure, safe is better than sorry. But this isn't true when it comes to breaking out of your inhibition zone.

Starting a conversation at the deli counter, asking someone for his/her phone number, or going to a wine-tasting class alone keeps you from looking back at your life and saying, "If only I had done it differently..." I know it's not easy, but the more you go down the "scary road," the easier it becomes—and the more you enrich your social life!

Roadblock Statement: "I Should Avoid Talking to Strangers"

Parents should certainly teach their small children this lesson. But for adults, talking to strangers can be great. You can practice your flirting skills and evaluate reactions. Think about some of your routine activities—food shopping, waiting in lines, sitting on the bus, browsing in a store, walking , traveling, and so on. Couldn't all of these situations benefit from a little conversation?

Talking to strangers is crucial to your flirting journey. What is the easiest conversation topic? It is what's going on around you. Practice this and it will become easy.

Roadblock Statement: "If I Wait Long Enough, Good Things Will Happen"

Who said that anyway? And how long is long enough? What a cop out this is!

Believing in this roadblock will give you false hope and will increase your chances of disappointment and sadness. Stop waiting! Make a plan, try something new, and take ownership of your life. It will feel so gratifying.

Imagine that you are the woman in the photo, who frequently crosses paths with a fellow runner she finds attractive. Instead of passively passing him by each week, make a plan to get his attention. Smile the next time you see him, quickly compliment him on his pace, or ask if he's training for a marathon. Often times we only get a single chance to meet someone who "happens to be running by us."

Roadblock Statement: "Women Who Approach Men Are Needy"

Quite the contrary is true. Women who approach men go after what they want and don't wait for Mr. Right to come to them (which, as we learned in the previous roadblock statement, doesn't work).

Men love when women approach them. I've heard this from hundreds of men of all ages. Not only is it an ego boost, but it's also oh-so-flattering. They only have one complaint. They wish women did it more frequently.

I know what you are saying—"I want him to come to me. Then I'll know that he likes me"—but does it really matter who approached whom? Why not give it a try? I have a feeling you'll be pleasantly surprised.

FROM THE FLIRTING FIELD

Nancy, a woman in her thirties, was on her way into the city for a job interview. She was standing on the train platform when Scott, also in his thirties, approached her to ask when the next train would arrive.

Nancy, who had just had a manicure, asked herself whether she should help this stranger—ruining her nails to get the schedule out—or just say she didn't know. Looking up at him warmly, she reached carefully into her briefcase. With a smile and a genuine laugh, she said, "I wouldn't ruin my nails for just anyone."

Scott smiled and thanked her, and the two continued talking. He asked her questions, showed interest, and moved a bit closer. They took the train together, continued talking, and by the end of the ride, had plans for that evening.

"MAKE A PLAN, TRY SOMETHING NEW, AND TAKE OWNERSHIP OF YOUR LIFE. IT WILL FEEL SO GRATIFYING."

Roadblock Statement: "Men Who Approach Women Only Want One Thing"

That is so right! But it's not what you think. Men want the same thing women do—to be liked and to make a meaningful connection.

Like women, men struggle with when and how to approach flirting interests, but they know the credo "Nothing ventured, nothing gained." Still, it is just as nerve-racking for men to approach women as it is for women to approach men. Ladies, give that brave guy a chance. He earned it.

(Yes, there will be guys who approach women for sex only, but that is not flirting—that's hitting on someone. And ladies, if this happens, simply say, "No thanks" and move away).

WHAT EVERY FLIRT SHOULD KNOW

Every person you flirt with isn't going to flirt back. Tell yourself, "So what! There are plenty of flirtees waiting for me."

Regardless of whether you are male or female, approximately one in three people with whom you flirt will flirt back. The good news is that the more you put yourself out there, the more positive results you will experience. The solution is to flirt more frequently.

Roadblock Statement: "Singles Events are the Only Places to Flirt"

Sure, singles events are great places to flirt, but don't limit yourself. Flirt anywhere and everywhere. The more you flirt, the better your chances for success. Sure, singles events are great places to flirt, but don't limit yourself. The more you flirt, the better your chances for success. And when the stakes are low (you are flirting for the enjoyment of it), the outcome can be serendipitous.

Take your high school reunion, for example. You may think it will only be fun for those popular in high school. Think again. High school reunions are great flirting grounds, as well as opportunities to reconnect with old friends, make new ones, and see what develops.

We often shy away from events where we feel we won't measure up to the other invited guests. Know that this fear comes from insecurity and not the situation's reality. You will come up with 101 reasons not to go, but none of them justifies missing a great opportunity to flirt with old—and new—flames.

"THE MORE YOU FLIRT, THE BETTER YOUR CHANCES FOR SUCCESS."

Roadblock Statement: "It's a Waste of Time to Attend a Party Where I Know Only the Host"

Attending a party where you only know one or two individuals is an incredible opportunity to meet and connect with new people. It gives you a chance to spread your wings. Take control of having fun!

You can accomplish this by changing your behavior from less of a guest to more of a host. Acting in a host-like manner will make it easier for you to talk to strangers. Try asking the following questions: "Have you tried the specialty drink?" or "Would you like my seat so you can eat? I know seats are scarce." or "You look cold . . . would you like to wear my jacket?" You'll come across as observant and interested in others' well-being.

Don't turn down invitations to parties where you don't know many guests. Instead, arrive early to be part of the welcoming committee. That way, you'll have more time to get comfortable, feel out the vibe, and get to know people at a relaxed pace.

Roadblock Statement: "Dining Alone Screams 'Loser'"

Dining alone is an enticement to flirt with those around you. Remember, it takes confidence to eat alone. It also says that you may desire a dining companion.

When dining alone, try the following tips:

- Propose to another lone diner that you eat together, particularly if there is a wait for tables. Tell your potential companion it will shorten the wait time.

- Comment to a flirting interest about the dish that s/he is eating. Say, "That looks really tasty. How is it?"

- Ask a flirting interest—maybe that cute waiter or waitress—to recommend something from the menu.

- Bring a book or magazine in case you feel uncomfortable. Props such as these (see page 182) make it easier for others to approach you. It provides a ready-made conversation topic. ("How is that book? I just picked up a copy yesterday.")

Roadblock Statement: "I Shouldn't Talk to Someone I Don't Know Until I Am Introduced"

What are you waiting for? Are you waiting for someone else to talk to that woman who you would like to meet, or for that man who's had his eye on you all night to make the first move? You could wait forever.

Wallflowers wallow, but flirters flourish. Be your own master of ceremonies and go for it. Put on a smile, stand up straight, extend your hand, and introduce yourself. This could be your flirting break! Take control of your social life. Nobody else will. You owe it to yourself.

TO FLIRT OR NOT TO FLIRT?

If you ask me, there's no reason *not* to flirt. Flirting is like warm chocolate chip cookies for the soul. It will sweeten your day, warm your heart, fuel your body, and put a smile on your face. It will turn boring, dull, stale conversations—or no conversation at all—into awe-inspiring, rousing discourse. Flirting will strengthen and rejuvenate your relationships. People will flock to you because you make them feel fabulous.

Think of flirting as a way to transform meeting new people into instant adventure, friendship, fun, and romance, and as a way to turn ordinary into unforgettable.

FLIRTING GOALS

If you understand the goals of flirting, you'll become a flirting pro in no time. Stay on course, have fun, and always remember that playing by the goals will bring you success.

FROM THE FLIRTING FIELD

Alyssa was meeting her friend Jen for a drink after work to share her good news of getting in to her dream graduate school. When Alyssa arrived, she noticed lots of single guys hanging out at the bar, so she took a seat and waited for Jen to arrive.

Brian came over to Alyssa and they started talking. Alyssa could not stop talking about her good news. She went on and on for about ten minutes, never once coming up for air or asking Brian a single question about himself. Finally, Brian glanced at his watch and said he had to get going. Alyssa could not figure out what went wrong.

During our next coaching session, Alyssa realized that she had not shown any interest in Brian and reminded herself that next time, she would need to "shine the spotlight" on her interest as well. She left confident that she would not make the same mistake again.

FLIRTING GOAL #1: SHINE THE SPOTLIGHT ON YOUR FLIRTING INTEREST, NOT ON YOURSELF

You want to make the other person feel special, cared about, important, and valued. Don't showcase yourself by doing all of the talking or trying to impress. Instead, focus on your flirting interest, letting him/her shine. (This also minimizes disappointment if your flirting interest does not reciprocate, as your goal was to simply make someone else feel special.) Once you have mastered that, you will experience the rewards of flirting.

FLIRTING GOAL #2: FLIRT FOR FUN, NOT TO GET A DATE OR PHONE NUMBER

Say what? Isn't the end goal to get a date or some digits?

No, it's not. I know it sounds crazy. In fact, when I tell my flirting students what I just told you, their jaws often drop. Some look ready to head for the door and demand their money back! But if you follow my advice, you will, in all likelihood, increase your chances astronomically of getting both—later.

TOP TEN REASONS TO FLIRT

In case you need some more concrete reasons to flirt, here it goes. Flirt because it:

1. Feels exhilarating
2. Boosts your ego
3. Makes others remember you
4. Brings new people into your life
5. Makes you more attractive
6. Acts as an icebreaker
7. Gets you noticed
8. Brings romance
9. Makes you a people magnet
10. Increases your chances of getting a date with someone you like

I know this sounds contradictory, but consider the following argument: The best flirting is spontaneous and focuses on the moment. The minute you focus on the future—phone number, date, and so on—you increase your anxiety level, you start to listen less and talk more, and your flirting ability diminishes, thereby lowering your chances of actually getting a date.

Trust me on this one. Thousands of flirting students agree that as much as they want that date, to get the most benefit, they have to stay in the moment and truly enjoy the process.

FLIRTING GOAL #3: MAKE FLIRTING SECOND NATURE

Flirting is a two-way pastime. Whether or not you return the flirting serve, it feels good to know that someone finds you attractive. Let the electricity grow as you flirt back and forth. Pay attention to the comfort level and interest of your flirting partner to guide your game. If you get the go-ahead, continue playing. If you try too hard and the ball is never in your court, pick up your racket and play with someone else.

Practice is important. Think of flirting as a sport. You would not expect to be a good tennis player, golfer, runner, ice skater, swimmer, or cyclist if you did not practice! Flirting—like any other sport—can be learned, tweaked, perfected, and customized until it feels natural.

SELF-CONFIDENCE: THE NUMBER ONE INGREDIENT FOR FABULOUS FLIRTING

Have you ever wondered about the single most important factor in being a fabulous flirt? Is it being drop-dead gorgeous, having a perfect body, or being a natural-born comedian? Is it having a little of each?

No, it's not any of these things. The number one flirting ingredient is confidence. Amazing flirts unequivocally believe they are worth getting to know. They have little fear about being rejected and make flirting look effortless. Confidence is a huge turn-on.

FIVE GREAT CONFIDENCE BOOSTERS

Does your self confidence need a quick lift? Here are five confidence boosters that will improve your flirting skills:

1. Call a friend. Caring friends or family will *ooh* and *ahh* at our slightest accomplishments, and are great at giving pep talks when you need them.

2. Be your own BFF (best friend forever). Feel good about your willingness and desire to flirt and be social. And enjoy yourself while doing it!

3. Help someone. Giving to others, in any form, will build your confidence in a huge way and make you more open to flirting.

4. Play with kids! Take your niece or nephew out for the day, or play some ball with your friend's kids in the backyard. They'll think you're the coolest grown-up ever, and you'll feel pretty great yourself.

5. Put a positive spin on everything you do. Need to clean your apartment? Think of it as a great way to "makeover" your space and appreciate the fresh look you'll be giving to the place. Use the same mentality at work, and on yourself.

THE FOUR-STEP PLAN TO BECOMING A CONFIDENT FLIRT

If you lack confidence, does it mean you are destined for flirting failure? Not at all! Here's an easy, four-step process I created to boost anyone's confidence.

Step #1: Look Your Best

When you look good, you feel good; when you look great, you feel great. Consider your appearance an investment in your flirting future.

Take a good look in the mirror. What can you do now to improve your look (forget about plastic surgery or losing weight overnight)? Ask a caring friend for some advice.

The following tips can help all of us:

- Fix that posture! Stand up straight with your shoulders back and your head held high. Don't look like a statue, but pay attention to how you carry yourself.
- Find glasses (if you wear them) that compliment your face. Avoid wearing sunglasses when flirting so your flirting interest can see your eyes.
- Make sure you are well-rested and well-groomed.

TIPS FOR THE WELL-GROOMED GUY

- Keep your nails clean and cut.
- Shave or trim all facial hair.
- Wear appropriate and clean foot gear; it speaks volumes about you.
- Don clothes and shoes appropriate to the occasion. Stock your closet with a few outfits that look really great on you and that you feel good wearing.
- Smell good. A clean smell is a major turn-on.
- Look like you tried to make a good impression.

TIPS FOR THE WELL-GROOMED GAL

- Have manicured nails whenever possible.
- Find a great hairdresser, or several (one for cut, one for color, one for hair emergencies), who you trust.
- Dress for the occasion.
- Use makeup as an enhancer, not a mask.
- Smell good but don't overdo the perfume.
- Spend a little more money on a few smashing outfits that make you feel great rather than spending less on outfits in which you feel so-so.

Step #2: Practice Confidence

Feeling confident and acting it are very different. Self-esteem is how you feel inside; self-confidence is how you present yourself to the world. Even if your self-esteem is a three or four on a scale of one to ten, rise above it and act *as if* it's a ten.

In other words, fake it until you make it. If you act like the most confident, self-assured person on the planet, others will respond to you more frequently and positively. This will, in turn, boost your self-esteem. Fake it enough, and your confidence may actually improve.

Practice in a mirror, or even better, practice in front of others. Role-play how you would act if you owned the room. By doing this, you become aware of which behaviors exude confidence.

Try these confident behaviors:

- Good posture
- Good eye contact
- Genuine smile
- Good listening
- Enthusiasm
- Open body language
- Poise
- Charm
- Warmth

FLIRTING TIP: PRACTICE A NEW CONFIDENT BEHAVIOR EACH DAY FOR A WEEK!

Another way to enhance your confidence is by practicing a single behavior each day for a week, so that you can concentrate on one behavior at a time. As your confidence grows, you will be able to naturally incorporate all these behaviors into your flirting repertoire.

- **Day 1:** Practice good posture as often as possible. Every time you feel yourself slouching, sit/stand up straight.
- **Day 2:** Practice making good eye contact whenever you are talking with someone.
- **Day 3:** Practice smiling as often as you can. Make sure it is a caring, genuine smile.
- **Day 4:** Listen as attentively as possible to everyone who talks to you.

- **Day 5:** Show authentic enthusiasm whenever possible.
- **Day 6:** Practice open body language (arms open, relaxed stance).
- **Day 7:** Practice poise, charm, and warmth by demonstrating sincere interest, politeness, and kindness to all of those around you.

Step #3: Demonstrate the Dynamic Duo: Chutzpah and Charm

Flirting combines chutzpah (pronounced HOOT-spuh) and charm.

Chutzpah often describes someone nervy and bold who isn't afraid to take risks. A dose of chutzpah gives you the confidence and permission to make the first move, start a conversation, test the waters, or break out of your comfort zone. Chutzpah also acts as a pick-me-up when your flirting interest says no thanks. Even if you don't *think* you have chutzpah, pretend you do. Again, fake it until you make it!

Charm combines charisma, warmth, and authenticity. Display charm, and you will draw people toward you, put them at ease, and make them feel welcome in your presence. They will want to hang out around you.

To be charming, do the following:

- Look your best.
- Accept compliments gracefully.
- Remember people's names.
- Give your flirting interest your undivided attention.
- Be empathetic.
- Dish out compliments freely and honestly.

The chemical reaction of chutzpah and charm transforms a shy, timid, withdrawn person into a confident, natural flirt. Consider this winning combination your secret flirting weapon. And remember that the more you use it, the better your flirting repertoire will be.

FROM THE FLIRTING FIELD

Carol, a fifty-year-old divorcee, was having trouble meeting men. After several sessions with me, Carol realized that she needed to inject a little chutzpah and charm into her flirting repertoire. For her first mission, she broke out of her comfort zone and started talking to the guy sitting next to her in jury duty. The results were immediate! He told her she made jury duty so interesting that he hoped to get called again.

Step #4: Create Your Flirting Energy

Flirting is less about what you say and more about the energy you create with your flirting interest. Playful banter, intense eye contact, curiosity, and undivided attention will create stimulating and exciting flirting energy.

To do this, focus on the other person and do whatever you can to make him/her feel special. Block out the rest of the world to establish a bond between you. This tempting energy will not only boost your confidence, but it will make your flirting interest yours before you know it.

WHAT FLIRTING IS *NOT*

Throughout this chapter, I've used many words to describe flirting, including *fun*, *playful*, *friendly*, and *nonthreatening*. There are many things, however, that flirting is *not*, and it's important to review them to avoid uncomfortable circumstances.

Flirting is not seduction. Seduction is clear and direct, coming on to someone in a sexual way.

With seduction, sex is the goal, and the person on the receiving end is the prey. It is a sure sign of seduction if during an initial encounter you feel uncomfortable, overpowered, uneasy, or fearful. You will know if someone is trying to seduce you. S/He will speak to you in a sexual way and will downplay the talk if you start asking questions. Trust your gut reaction, which is probably telling you to get away as fast as you can.

Real flirts know the difference between seduction and flirting, and they never mix flirting with sexual come-ons.

Flirting is not manipulative. Genuine flirting is not about trying to make yourself feel good or trying to get something you want at another person's expense. These intentions and behaviors are disingenuous and deceptive. This is not flirting; it's manipulation.

Real flirts are always sincere, truthful, and honest and are genuinely interested in their flirting prospects. They have a knack for making their flirting interest feel as if s/he is the only person in the room.

Flirting is not a power play. In a power play, one person wants control at all times, to be the top dog. This is evident, for example, when that person must have the last word, uses insulting sarcasm, denigrates anything the flirting interest says, and only wants to hear his/her own voice.

Real flirts care about others and share the power and energy.

Flirting is not dishonest. Fake flirts thoroughly win over their flirting interest only to swiftly discard that person and move on to the next subject. An example is the bar queen who pretends to want every guy at the bar only to quickly discard each as soon as he shows interest or buys her a drink. Her only goal is to conquer and move on. She has no regrets.

Real flirts are trustworthy, straightforward, and scrupulous. They say what they mean and they mean what they say.

FROM BABY BOOMERS TO SOCIALLY SHY: FLIRTING IS FOR EVERYONE

That means you! Regardless of age, background, or situation, everybody flirts (some better than others!), and it makes us all feel good. Flirting is simply about being comfortable in your own skin.

We all come to the flirting field with our battle scars (our unique life experiences), but flirting can work for boomers, divorcées, widows, shy people—anyone. At any stage of life, turn your lemons into lemonade. You can't change the past, but you can make today a flirting sensation.

ARE YOU SOCIALLY SHY AND SCARED TO FLIRT?

Apprehension about flirting is so common. Almost everyone fears the rejection, even if just a little. But it does little good to worry about it, so why not focus on how to overcome it? Feeling well-equipped will lessen the doubts. Here are some tips to minimize trepidation and make flirting easier:

- Tell yourself that flirting is merely being friendly.
- Rehearse opening lines you can use and reuse (see page 154 for examples).
- Watch the news or read the newspaper so you can sound in-the-know about world events.
- Rehearse open-ended questions that you can adapt to a variety of situations. My favorites including asking someone about his/her free time, name (if it's unique), or greatest desires if money were no object.
- Don't be afraid to tell your flirting interest that you are a bit nervous about making the first move. It could be a great ice breaker.
- Take mini flirting steps. Tell yourself that you will flirt at least once a week, or you will flirt whenever you are waiting in line or at the bus stop and see someone who seems interesting.

The best way to overcome the fear of flirting is to take a risk and flirt. By doing so, you will decrease your anxiety and increase your opportunity to be successful. Think of it as just being sociable, outgoing, and good company.

ARE YOU A YOUNG WOMAN TOO EMBARRASSED TO FLIRT?

Many young women believe they should not have to flirt, incorrectly assuming that men "just know" they are single and interested. "I shouldn't have to work hard at meeting a guy," I hear them say. "I am young, attractive, and have a good personality. I just feel funny flirting. It's not me."

Here's my advice: Guys aren't mind-readers and need signs from you showing it is okay to walk over to you, talk to you, and possibly ask for your phone number. Your "signs" don't have to take you too far outside of your comfort zone either—try making eye contact or giving a small smile.

Although you may feel embarrassed, focus on having a good time, complimenting, and not worrying about the outcome. Think of flirting as your free ticket to meeting a really nice guy.

ARE YOU DIVORCED AND FEEL CLUELESS ABOUT FLIRTING?

Whether you were married for four years or forty, divorce scars the psyche and can turn your life upside down, cause you to doubt yourself, and leave you feeling hurt, angry, lonely, cheated, worthless, or all of the above. You may feel out of place in a couples' world and will have to make new single friends.

Flirting can act as a baby step in the right direction, helping you practice connecting with others and boosting your self-esteem. The more positive results you get, the more you'll want to flirt. It may feel awkward and strange initially, but if you persevere, it will surely become enjoyable and rewarding.

ARE YOU WIDOWED AND FEEL OUT OF PLACE FLIRTING?

After the death of a spouse—when you're ready, of course—flirting is a way to connect with those around you and bring new people into your life. Because loss of a spouse can also mean losing your social circle, flirting helps fill the void and helps you start anew. Remember, widowhood only defines you if you allow it to.

When flirting with a stranger, remember s/he is flirting with you, not your marital status. Let flirting lift your spirits, distract you from your grief, and add some joy to your life.

ARE YOU A NEW COLLEGE STUDENT WHO FINDS FLIRTING AWKWARD?

College is exciting, adventurous, and overwhelming at once. Everything is new and different and you have to make new friends. Your best friend attends a school three states away, your other friends are scattered across the country, and your family is no longer at your disposal.

Use flirting to acclimate to your new life away from home. Other students like yourself will be so happy you made the first move that you'll get much attention in return. You have so many places to flirt, too: in class, in the dorm, at the local hot spots, at student activities and parties, in the library, at the student center, online, and so on.

ARE YOU A PERSON WITH SPECIAL NEEDS WHO FEELS SELF-CONSCIOUS ABOUT FLIRTING?

Do you have a medical condition or disability that makes you feel self-conscious about flirting? If so, remember that you are a person *with* an illness—you are not the illness.

When flirting, try not to talk about your illness or disability during your initial encounter, just like you would avoid subjects such as your ex-spouse, how much money you make, how much debt you owe, or any other personal topics. If your disability is visible and your flirting interest asks, talk about it briefly, but don't let it dominate the conversation. Remember that you have much to offer and that your condition is only a piece of you. Remind others of the same.

Everyone comes to relationships with limitations. Remember that your attitude says the most about you—let the real you shine through, and everything else will take a back seat.

ARE YOU A BABY BOOMER UNSURE ABOUT FLIRTING?

Most Baby Boomers have been in at least one long-term relationship and bring age and experience to the flirting table. This is a major plus!

Think of flirting as a fun, care-free activity and as a way to bring companionship and friendship into your life. Flirting can lead to all sort of activities: going out to dinner or to a movie; finding a traveling companion, tennis partner, or date; or starting a new chapter in your life. Devote some time each day to flirting. You won't regret it!

PART ONE

YOUR MOVE-BY-MOVE GUIDE TO THE
BODY LANGUAGE OF FLIRTING

Did you know that 90 percent of communication is nonverbal?
Everything you do—your gestures, posture, facial expressions, eye
contact, smile, tone of voice, and so on—affect what message you
convey. Your nonverbal communication speaks volumes and is
even more convincing than the actual words you speak. It communicates your thoughts and feelings about yourself and the person
with whom you are flirting or with whom you want to flirt.

You should understand body-language nuances and nonverbal
communication secrets before you embark on your flirting journey. This section shows you how to read between the lines, for
your benefit and that of your flirting interest. Nine simple moves
will arm you with the tools to wow those lucky people you'll now
be able to meet.

Consider me your flirting coach. I will guide you through this
nonverbal maze and offer practical tips to help you stand out
in a crowd, feel less self-conscious, take more control, and feel
more confident about finding love. Now let's get started!

MOVE ONE

SMILE TO MAKE YOURSELF MORE APPROACHABLE AND ATTRACTIVE

A smile is to flirting what air is to breathing. Without it, flirting is impossible. The radiance and warmth a smile emanates sets the stage for a great flirtatious encounter.

Smiling is one of the most effective ingredients in your flirting repertoire. It makes you more approachable and attractive. It lights up your face. It truly changes your appearance. Smiling draws people in and makes them feel welcome. People who frown, grimace, or appear depressed or angry at the world turn people off. A genuine smile says, "I like you, I accept you, I will not hurt you, and yes, I want to meet you."

Studies have shown that when asked who they find most attractive, both men and women select pictures of smiling people. It is not about attractiveness but approachability; the more approachable you are, the greater your chances will be of connecting with a romantic partner.

Imagine yourself at a party, café, or bar. In these situations, you may either want to get noticed, find someone you would like to meet, or both. Smiling, the perfect avenue to facilitate these goals, makes the approach so much easier (for both parties) and removes some of the situational anxiety.

Men see a woman's smile as an immediate invitation to approach her without the fear of rejection. Women see a man's smile as a signal that he wants her to approach him.

THE RIGHT WAY TO SMILE FOR BEST RESULTS

The way you smile sends a powerful message. A fast smile that quickly drops back to no smile communicates insincerity. Your smile should seem natural, relaxed, and genuine. A smile is the universal signal for friendliness and should reflect that.

If smiling makes you self-conscious, pay attention to your reaction when a stranger smiles at you. Do you feel uncomfortable or like the most important person on the planet?

Practice Makes (a Smile) Perfect

If smiling at people feels unnatural or you want to improve your smiling game, practice smiling at people during everyday encounters. For example, smile while doing the following:

- Walking your dog
- Waiting for a bus
- Standing in line at the supermarket (or anywhere, for that matter)
- Filling your car's tank with gas
- Dining in a restaurant
- Walking around the office
- Sitting in class

FROM THE FLIRTING FIELD

Look at the person for approximately two to four seconds, smile, look away, and then continue on your way. This activity puts you more at ease smiling at strangers so it becomes second nature. Remember, there are no strings attached. You do not have to start a conversation; just smile. Practice this technique five times a day for two weeks. The more you do it, the easier it becomes.

EIGHT REASONS TO SMILE

Why should you smile? Though many reasons exist, here are eight, for starters. Smiling:

1. Makes you adorable
2. Is contagious
3. Makes you feel good
4. Relaxes you
5. Keeps you positive
6. Is a natural drug
7. Makes you confident
8. Makes you approachable

FROM THE FLIRTING FIELD

Marissa, a thirty-four-year-old divorced woman, was amazed at how quickly she overcame her fear of smiling at strangers. "After my divorce, I was clueless about how to meet a guy," she said. "I was with my husband since I was twenty-four and I was just overwhelmed being

MOVE TWO

MAKE EYE CONTACT TO ESTABLISH TRUST AND INTIMACY

Imagine seeing a cute guy or gal across the room or at a clothing shop. Now what do you do? You could look away and then kick yourself when s/he leaves. You could wait for him/her to come over to you, which may never happen. Isn't there a better way? Yes, there is! Here is an opportunity to test the romantic waters, break out of your comfort zone, and meet someone new.

To show him/her that you have noticed and that s/he has captured your attention, bat your baby blues and look directly into the other person's eyes.

EYE CONTACT REVEALS SELF-CONFIDENCE

Eye contact is the soul of flirtation. It establishes trust and intimacy. Making eye contact is a great way to introduce yourself to your interest.

Eye contact should last two to four seconds. Anything longer will cause the other person to feel uncomfortable. Making eye contact is a sign of self-confidence, which is a real turn-on.

Often our feelings of diminished self-esteem prevent us from making eye contact, but we must overcome this, as the very act of looking someone in the eye communicates our willingness to take a risk and our feelings about the other person. Remember, you are worth it, and the more you show this to others, the greater your odds of success.

"ACTING SELF-CONFIDENT CAN BOOST YOUR CONFIDENCE FOR REAL. FAKE IT UNTIL YOU MAKE IT! IT REALLY WORKS."

NERVOUS? FLIRT WITH YOUR FRIENDS FIRST!

Practicing eye contact with strangers can feel daunting. Practicing with people familiar to you can make you more confident in your ability to do this well and reinforce its importance in your flirting repertoire.

Using a simple set of exercises (listed below), practice eye contact with a friend. Seated face to face, try the following, without speaking:

1. Look your partner in the eye while s/he looks down or away from you. Do this for one minute.
2. Reverse roles and repeat.
3. Finally, make direct eye contact with your partner for five- and ten-second intervals.

How did you react in each of these situations? When eye contact wasn't reciprocated, did you feel unimportant? When it was maintained, were you more at ease? Keep in mind these emotions next time you're gazing with a stranger.

YOUR EYES SAY IT ALL

Did you know that your eyes flirt independently? You blink more frequently and your pupils dilate when you come in contact with someone you like.

SIX TECHNIQUES FOR GIVING THE BEST "FLIRTING EYE"

To become a pro at making eye contact, you must practice, practice, and practice some more. Whatever you do and wherever you are, make eye contact: in an elevator, a bookstore, a restaurant, a class, on the street, in a church or temple, in a park—anywhere.

Use the half-dozen techniques below interchangeably or in conjunction with one another, in situations in which you'd like to meet the eyes of a stranger.

Technique #1: Glance, Then Look Away

Glance at your flirting interest for one to two seconds and then look away. Repeat several times. Once you've mastered this, glance at your interest for two to three seconds and then look away. Repeat several times.

Use this move when in a large group, when across the room from your flirting interest, or during situations that require silence (e.g., a lecture or religious event).

Technique #2: Smile and Glance

Smile and glance at your flirting interest for one or two seconds. Repeat several times. Once you feel comfortable, smile and glance for three seconds and then look away. Use a shy smile or one that reaches your eyes and lights up your face. An open smile shows genuine affection and heightened interest. Go for it.

CHART YOUR EYE CONTACT PROGRESS

Consider keeping a looking log in which you chart your successes and identify situations that require additional practice. Your log may look something like this:

- **Date:** June 14th
- **Time:** 2:30 p.m.
- **Location:** Bookstore
- **Lookee:** Cute guy with plaid coat and glasses
- **Feelings:** Nervous, yet eager to approach him
- **Action:** Although I was scared to death, I decided to follow Fran's advice and take a risk. While walking toward him, I made eye contact and even mustered up the energy to smile.
- **Lookee's response:** Mr. Adorable guy looked my way and I think he even smiled back.
- **Final thoughts and feelings:** I wish I would have said something or didn't continue walking. The next time I want to approach someone, I will say something. At least I had the courage to look and smile.

Technique #3: Use the Darting Eye Glance (DEG)

Men love performing the DEG. They look at a woman, look away, look again, and look away. It all happens quickly; one round of four DEGs takes no more than five seconds.

The man often does this without thought when a woman he wants to meet mesmerizes him. If you receive the DEG, volley back with a smile and a glance and slowly move closer to him.

FLIRTING TIP: USE THE EYE CONTACT TRICK

If you find looking at someone directly in the eye too overwhelming, try focusing your eye contact on the person's forehead or chin. This action gives your flirting partner the impression of eye contact, especially from afar.

Technique #4: Try the Look Down Technique (LDT)

Women are experts at the LDT. They look at a man for one second and then immediately look down. They repeat this several times. Any guy lucky enough to receive the LDT can be 100 percent sure this woman wants his attention.

If you receive the LDT, opportunity is knocking at your door. Respond with an open smile and make great eye contact as you make your way over to talk.

Technique #5: Put on Your Bedroom Eyes

Can you use bedroom eyes outside of the bedroom? Yes, it is absolutely, positively possible! Why do it? Because bedroom eyes are irresistible and appealing any time of the day.

When you spot someone you like, let your pupils unfocus by staring at the floor or ceiling for a minute or two without blinking. Those minutes may feel like forever, but hang in there. When time's up, blink three times. Your eyes will water just a bit, and your pupils will dilate—and you'll look absolutely alluring!

TRY BEDROOM EYES WITH A FRIEND

Practice this technique with someone who also wants to enhance his/her flirting skills. In no time, you'll transform your everyday eyes into tempting, enthralling eyes.

FROM THE FLIRTING FIELD

Sean, a thirty-year-old student in my flirting workshop, became mesmerized by his thirty-two-year-old partner Paula's eyes. "Fran instructed us to look at the person's eyes next to us,"

"WINKING AT SOMEONE ESTABLISHES, IN A NONVERBAL WAY, A SPECIAL BOND BETWEEN YOU."

Technique #6: Wink for Real Impact

Want an effortless way to create intimacy? Try winking. It takes only a second, creates a sense of camaraderie between winker and winkee, and is playful and sexy.

Winking at someone establishes, in a nonverbal way, a special bond between you. Men today have forgotten the dreamy tenderness associated with winking. This simple action, once considered in the male domain, has become gender-neutral. Women can affect any man by winking in a warm, gentle way. A woman who winks at a guy will make a lasting impression. A wink coupled with a winning smile is even better.

A perfect wink happens just once. Look at your flirting interest, get his/her attention, and quickly close one eyelid (whichever eye feels most comfortable and natural).

To practice before taking your wink "to the streets," try winking at yourself in the mirror or asking a friend to wink at you (and winking back).

WINKING NO-NOS

- Don't accompany your wink with "Oh baby, baby" and stare at the person from head to toe.
- Don't stare at a person's body parts (other than his/her eyes) after you wink.
- Do not wink with both eyes. It says that you have something in your eye.

FROM THE FLIRTING FIELD

Desiree, a shy fifty-year-old Bostonian, loved the idea of winking. Recalling her experiences getting winked at made her smile. But the thought of *her* winking at a guy seemed terrifying. "I could never do that; it just seemed too pushy," she said.

But Desiree wanted to overcome her fear, so she decided to practice winking at the kids in her neighborhood. Their giggles and acceptance gave her the confidence to try it with men, who were more than receptive to it!

EYE CONTACT DON'TS

When we feel uneasy or unsure about approaching someone, we overcompensate, try too hard, or do whatever we can to alleviate our nerves. Sometimes we stare for so long that the person feels embarrassed and uncomfortable. Or we go to the other extreme and avoid any eye contact at all. These behaviors typically backfire because in attempting to ease our own discomfort, we actually push the person away. Prolonged eye contact can be perceived as threatening or intrusive, while passive eye contact—or no eye contact at all—can convey disinterest and dishonesty. Although you might not mean to communicate these things, your eyes are doing the talking.

Remember, eye contact should feel friendly and relaxed and never come across as aggressive, hostile, intrusive, passive, or disinterested. "Easy on the eyes" is more than a great saying—it's a great tip too!

FLIRTING TIP: PUT ASIDE THE NERVES

Do you ever feel nervous, get sweaty palms, or freeze up when you spot someone interesting? You are not alone! We all feel that way. At times like these, take a deep breath, relax your mind, and remind yourself that "Andrew" or "Tracy" will be flattered that you have noticed him/her. Remember, you're just making eye contact and smiling. If you get no response, no problem; simply feel proud that you moved first.

FROM THE FLIRTING FIELD

Thirty-three-year-old Joel desperately wanted an introduction to thirty-year-old Marie, an acquaintance of his roommate Steve. Steve arranged a meeting at the local pub. Joel arrived early, sat at the bar, and eagerly waited for Marie. When she arrived, she came in and introduced herself to Joel, but he never looked her in the eye. When they did talk, he seemed focused on everything but her. After an hour, Joel asked Marie for her phone number. Marie declined. Joel was devastated.

Later, Joel asked Steve whether he knew the reason for Marie's response. Reluctantly Steve replied, "Marie didn't think you were interested because you never looked at her." Joel emailed Marie to explain that he was interested, but he just felt nervous that night. He apologized and the two decided to have dinner.

This story had a happy ending, but remember, we don't often get a second chance.

MOVE THREE

USE THE FLIRTATIOUS HANDSHAKE TO MAKE AN UNFORGETTABLE FIRST IMPRESSION

Most of us know the traditional business handshake. It requires a firm squeeze, lasts for about three seconds, and entails limited eye contact. Immediately after the handshake ends, you rarely remember that any physical contact has occurred (minus those unfortunate instances when an overzealous man crushes his partner's hand or a woman pinches her partner's fingers with her jewelry).

The flirtatious handshake is none of those things. Rather, it is the most playful, interesting move you can have in your flirting cupboard. Once you master it, you will unquestionably make an unforgettable first impression. Let me explain how.

The flirtatious handshake captivates your flirting interest because the connection comes from your smile, your eyes, and an engaging touch that leaves the recipient speechless—just for a moment—and eager to get to know you.

HOW TO DO THE FEMALE FLIRTATIOUS HANDSHAKE

Ladies, here are five steps to learn this fun, flirty handshake. Take a deep breath, stand up straight, and know that you are worth it! As you approach that charming guy, do the following (in the order listed below):

- Smile.
- Look directly into his eyes.
- Move in toward him and extend your right hand to initiate a handshake.
- With your right hand, shake his right hand with a firm grip. Simultaneously, using your left hand, quickly, softly, and gently stroke the back of his hand (the one you're holding).
- Say hello and introduce yourself with energy and sparkle.

WHY SHOULD YOU USE THIS HANDSHAKE?

Why use this inviting handshake instead of the polite, standard business one? Because it communicates to your interest the following:

- I want to wow you.
- I dare to be unique.
- I want you to know that I have really noticed you.
- I have a great sense of humor.
- I am not afraid to take a risk.

Like with all flirtation tools, the more you do this handshake, the more easily it will come to you and the more comfortable you will feel using it. Add your own sense of style, have fun with it, and remember to keep it lighthearted and playful.

HOW TO DO THE MALE FLIRTATIOUS HANDSHAKE

Guys, here are five easy steps to learn this enticing handshake. Remember, confidence is your ticket to success. As you approach that spectacular woman, do the following (in the order listed below):

- Smile.
- Look directly into her eyes.
- Move in toward her and extend your right hand to initiate a handshake.
- With your right hand, shake her right hand as you normally would. Simultaneously, bring your left hand into the shake and give an extra squeeze to the back of her hand (the one you're holding). Think of your hands as the bread of a sandwich, with her hand as the filling.
- Say hello and state how nice it is to meet her.

FROM THE FLIRTING FIELD

Joey, a twenty-four-year-old law student, often felt awkward and self-conscious around women to whom he was attracted. He never knew what to do with his hands. They always seemed to dangle and fidget.

"The male flirtatious handshake made me feel so charming and smooth," he said. "When

"LIKE WITH ALL FLIRTATION TOOLS, THE MORE YOU DO THIS HANDSHAKE, THE MORE EASILY IT WILL COME TO YOU AND THE MORE COMFORTABLE YOU WILL FEEL USING IT."

MOVE FOUR

MAINTAIN PROPER DISTANCE AND SPACE TO GET CLOSE

Have you ever found yourself literally backing up as someone talks in your face? You do it instinctively to re-establish comfortable boundaries. "How annoying," you think—and how mind-boggling that the "close talker" doesn't get the hint.

But the close talker has much to teach about how close really is too close. Here's a rule of thumb: A fabulous flirt never gets closer than an arm's length from his/her flirting interest.

Personal space can be best described as an invisible bubble that surrounds you. The bubble's size varies based on your own comfort zone, culture, and the situation. When someone gets too close, your personal space feels violated and you experience a physical and emotional reaction—you become tense, anxious, or uncomfortable, and you back away.

When you invade someone else's space, that person will likely react similarly and will do whatever necessary to maintain comfort and safety. Getting too close, no matter how innocent the behavior, can turn someone off—exactly the opposite effect you hope of your flirting.

SIGNS THAT YOU'RE TOO CLOSE FOR COMFORT

How do you know that you are too close? Back up a bit if your flirting interest does any of the following:

- Leans back in his/her chair
- Leans back, steps back, or makes an abrupt exit, leaving you perplexed
- Looks over you to avoid eye contact
- Folds his/her arms
- Leans his/her chin down and scrunches his/her shoulders into the neck

Always remember the goal of flirting: to make the other person feel special, comfortable, and interested in you—not scared off. If your flirting interest gives off any of these signs, take a full step back and reassess the situation.

SECRET FLIRTING ZONES: THE KEY TO MAINTAINING PROPER DISTANCE

Great flirts always pay attention to the following four flirting zones. Like the street signs of flirting, the zones keep you on track, win over your flirting interest, and ultimately bring you closer because you respect the other person's space.

Remember, it is much better to get invited closer than get pushed away!

Zone #1: The Do-Not-Flirt Zone

This first zone is the space eighteen inches (46 cm) out from your body, space normally reserved for whispering, hugging, or getting cheek to cheek.

As such, this is an absolute no-no for first-time flirters. If you enter this zone, you will likely get the boot before you can say a word. It's great to get cozy, but not with someone you met just twenty minutes ago.

Zone #2: The Perfect Flirting Zone

This zone, approximately eighteen inches (46 cm) to four feet (1.2 m) from your interest, marks the perfect flirting distance. You can easily see each other's nonverbal cues (which we discuss in more detail in moves seven and eight) and allows you to comfortably talk, make eye contact, and get noticed.

When approaching someone, start at the outskirts of zone #2, or three to four feet (1 to 1.2 m) away. As the flirting encounter progresses, slowly move in closer—but only when it feels right and your flirting interest gives you cues, such as saying, "I'm having trouble hearing you," or leaning in toward you.

Zone #3: The Flirting-at-a-Distance Zone

The third zone, four to ten feet (1.2 to 3 m) away from your flirting interest, equals flirting across the room or street. Your flirting moves must speak volumes to get you noticed in this zone. But it is possible. Make eye contact, send over a drink, wink, smile, and eventually make your way to the person who sparked your interest.

FLIRTING TIP: KNOW YOUR NO-ZONE

To figure out your own space boundaries, have a friend walk toward you. When you feel uncomfortable, have him/her stop. The distance between you and your friend is your comfort zone. Everyone's boundaries differ, so return the favor and have your friend give it a try.

Flirting Zone #4: The Out-of-Bounds Flirting Zone

Flirting from afar—ten to twenty-five feet (3 to 7.6 m) away—is challenging and not usually a flirting zone of choice. But if you're stuck with it, be innovative in getting someone's attention—a gentle wave, a big smile coupled with a wink, or several glances as you slowly move closer.

FROM THE FLIRTING FIELD

Jenn, twenty-two, and Ashley, nineteen, two college students who attended my seminar, recounted for our class a recent too-close-for-comfort incident they experienced.

As they were seated just the two of them at a long table in the college library, a male student approached rather suddenly, catching them off guard. Without asking, he sat down in the seat next to Jenn (despite twelve vacant seats at the table) and attempted conversation. Jenn felt uncomfortable and weird; Ashley found it comical and peculiar. Both considered it a big turn-off.

MOVE FIVE

SPEAK WITH APPROPRIATE BODY LANGUAGE TO STAND OUT

Frequently, flirting begins before either party speaks a single word. The right body language can spark interest, attraction, and acceptance; the wrong body language can trigger discomfort, dislike, or rejection. You probably know people with a knack for making you feel special and comfortable. You probably know others who quickly make you feel self-conscious, uneasy, and unworthy. You intuitively react to their body language, which then translates into how you feel about yourself and the other person. It just happens.

By learning how to read and control body language, however, you can ensure that you give off signals that communicate to others your authenticity, comfort, warmth, charisma, and playfulness. Fitting flirting body language is a passport to flirting paradise.

Not only that, but you'll also better know when your interest doesn't reciprocate feelings—an enormous long-term benefit that will save you time, energy, and heartache. (You just have to trust me on that one, no matter how much you want to disregard the warning signs!)

NEGATIVE BODY LANGUAGE: WHAT NOT TO DO

Before I tell you the perfect body language formula, let's go over what *not* to do, what I like to call "The Ultimate Body Language Don'ts," or BLDs. This list may look long, but we do many of these behaviors habitually and without knowing it. Sometimes, we even do these things *on purpose* to indicate to others that we're not interested—so be on the lookout on all accounts! Don't follow these bad habits, and don't waste your time with people who do.

Remember, BLDs distract, turn people off, are unattractive, and stand in your way. Once you know what not to do, discard the BLDs and replace them with positive body language. The more you know what not to do, the better flirt you will be.

The Ultimate Body Language Don'ts

Never do any of the following:

- **Look around the room when talking**
- Fold your arms across your chest in a tight, clenched manner
- Stand with one arm crossed tightly hugging the other arm
- **Stand or sit in a slumped position**
- Stand like a statue
- Look at the floor when talking
- Huddle in a smaller position
- Wrap your legs around each other
- Twist your feet around table or chair legs
- Put barriers in front of you such as a book, your arms, or a table
- **Play with or check your cell phone**

- Jiggle or twitch your knee or legs
- Fidget
- Tap your fingers on the table
- Pick at your skin
- Rub your nose
- Pick on your nails or cuticles
- Sigh, yawn, or rub your throat
- Frown or grimace
- Stare
- Clench your fists or shake your finger
- Wring your hands
- Shake your head from left to right as if to say "no"
- **Move in too quickly**
- Twirl your hair
- Nod a mile a minute
- Rub your arms and legs

- Shake hands with a limp handshake
- Speak in a monotone or so low that your partner can't hear you
- Speak in a loud arrogant tone
- Keep a smile plastered to your face
- **Glance at your watch**
- Bite your lip
- Laugh excessively (or at inappropriate times)
- Wear your heart on your sleeve
- Shred your dinner napkin
- Adjust your clothing constantly
- **Lean way back or away from the other person in your chair**
- Hide in the corner
- Shuffle your feet

"THE MORE YOU KNOW WHAT NOT TO DO, THE BETTER FLIRT YOU WILL BE."

Turn Your Wrongs Into Rights

Now that you know the BLDs, what's next? First, take a self-inventory of your own personal BLDs. How often do you display them and in what situations?

For most BLDs, simply don't do them. For some, do the opposite. For example, instead of slouching, stand up straight. Instead of glancing at your watch, make eye contact with your conversation partner. When you start mumbling or speaking too low, speak up.

Body language comes in clusters. Occasionally, you can yawn, adjust clothing, sigh, or make a nervous gesture, but don't make a habit out of it. Rather, look at the total picture.

WARNING SIGNS YOUR FLIRTING INTEREST IS NOT INTO YOU

Take a hint if your interest does the following:

- Looks around the room or at his/her watch when talking to you
- Doesn't ask you anything about yourself
- Boasts about him/herself
- Shakes his/her head from left to right or nods a mile a minute
- Yawns or fidgets
- Constantly interrupts you
- Moves away from you or is inattentive

POSITIVE BODY LANGUAGE: SPEAK WITH WELCOMING AND INVITING MOVEMENTS

Now that we've covered what *won't* work, are you ready to learn how to speak with body language to get noticed? Let's get started.

The right body language makes others feel comfortable around you and shows others you feel comfortable with yourself. The more you practice the steps outlined, the more success you will have when meeting new people.

Step #1: Take a Deep Breath

When you want to make a good impression or approach someone, do you get totally nervous? We all do; it's unavoidable. Taking some deep breaths helps.

Breathe in slowly and deeply through your nose until you can't take in any more air. Let out the air slowly and gently through your mouth. Repeat this two or three times. It reduces the jitters.

Step #2: Face the Person Directly and Make Eye Contact

When engaged in conversation, face the person to whom you are speaking. This sends the message that you are totally focused. In situations during which it is physically difficult to face each other, such as a crowded party, event, or waiting area, angle your body toward your partner as much as possible. We do this with people we find attractive.

Next, focus your eyes. Calm, friendly eye contact works best. Nothing is more distracting than squinting or straining eyes. It makes your face look lopsided and askew (try it in the mirror if you don't believe me). Keep your eyes open and alluring and don't forget to blink.

FLIRTING TIP: RELAX YOUR MOUTH (EXCEPT FOR SMILES AND LAUGHS)

Clenching or gritting your teeth sends a message of terror, fear, or anxiety. Some of us clench our teeth without realizing it. As soon as you feel your teeth touching, release the clench. All you have to do is pay more attention to it.

"THE RIGHT BODY LANGUAGE MAKES OTHERS FEEL COMFORTABLE AROUND YOU AND SHOWS OTHERS YOU FEEL COMFORTABLE WITH YOURSELF."

Step #3: Lean In

Leaning toward the person with whom you're speaking conveys your interest in spending time with and getting to know each other. When you lean in, you block out the world and say that only s/he matters. Try leaning in, talking, and then leaning in a little more.

FROM THE FLIRTING FIELD

Jill and Aaron, two thirty-somethings, met through Match.com. During the first ten minutes of their initial in-person meeting at a coffee shop, Aaron was leaning back in his chair. Jill was unsure whether Aaron was interested. As soon as he leaned forward and put his arms on the table, however, the vibe changed. Jill knew he was interested. They ended up going out for dinner the following night.

Step #4: Display Welcoming Arms

Have your arms in an open position—that is, relaxed at your sides. They don't have to remain completely still, but they should make only smooth, natural moves. Avoid crossing your arms or clutching them tightly against your body. This closed position makes others think you aren't interested in conversation (even if you really are). Arms in an open position tell others that you would like them to join you.

During conversation, move your arms easily and slowly away from your body, with palms up, to indicate agreement or interest in what your flirting partner says or does.

Step #5: Tilt Your Head

Tilting your head toward your partner during conversation says that you really want to hear what that person has to say. This will be an ego boost for your flirting interest, and in turn, s/he will likely let his/her guard down and feel more relaxed. Body language is all about reducing anxiety, increasing spontaneity, and focusing on the moment.

Step #6: Listen Attentively

Try to ignore distractions and concentrate on the conversation. The best way to listen atten-tively is to nod every few seconds, making comments such as "uh huh," "mmm," "yes, definitely," "absolutely," and so on—in a natural way.

It may sound like a no-brainer, but it guarantees great results. There is no better feeling than knowing that someone truly hears you.

And guys, nod more! Women love it.

FLIRTING TIP: IGNORE YOUR CELL PHONE

Pop quiz: Your cell phone rings, vibrates in your pocket, or buzzes with a text message alert. What do you do?

   a. Sneak a peek.
   b. Rush to answer it.
   c. Ignore it.
   d. Ignore it and say, "Sorry for the interruption."
   e. Quickly text back.

If you answered d, bravo! This best communicates that you find the other person more important and interesting than anyone calling. Now that's flirting!

Step #7: Offer Your Undivided Attention

Because people today don't want to waste a second, simultaneously talking, texting, eating, and walking seems like normal behavior. But during a first-time meeting, it's imperative you give that person your exclusive attention. Consider the following story.

Paula and Christopher, two people in their late twenties, met at a bike race. During registration, Christopher started complimenting Paula's biking outfit, telling her how put-together she looked. Paula immediately felt a connection.

However, as the conversation progressed, Christopher began texting and waving to all of the women from his bike club. Because of the mixed, multitasked messages Paula received from Christopher, she took off.

After the race, Christopher approached Paula, said he was glad he ran into her, and asked her to lunch. She agreed, but during lunch, she explained to Christopher her surprise at his interest in her. He appeared more interested in texting and saying hi to his biking buddies than talking to her, she said. Christopher apologized and said he didn't even realize what he had done.

Lesson learned: Multitasking gives the impression that other "tasks" take precedence over the person to whom you are talking. Remember, we all want to be the center of the universe. Pay full attention. You won't regret it.

FLIRTING TIP: PERFECT YOUR BODY LANGUAGE TO SPARK ATTRACTION

Perk up your body vibes with these ten tips:

1. Smile and laugh.
2. Relax your body.
3. Make eye contact.
4. Stand tall and sit up straight.
5. Use your hands to show confidence.
6. Avoid touching your face.
7. Do not fidget.
8. Uncross your arms.
9. Think positively.
10. Stop the BLDs (for more on the BLDs, see page 76).

Step #8: Use the Most Truthful Part of Your Body

Actions clearly speak louder than words. If a person agrees to call or meet up and then doesn't call or show up, you know there's no longer interest (or maybe that there never was). Actions are much more important than empty words. But one body part never lies. Do you know which one?

a. Face

b. Eyes

c. Arms

d. Feet/legs

e. Fingers

If you guessed d, you are absolutely right! We can hide our emotions in all body parts except for our feet/legs. Some experts believe that because our feet are the farthest body part from the brain, they don't think—they just *do*. Here's what it means to us flirty flirts: We point our legs toward our interest. Otherwise, we point our legs away. If you can't decide whether s/he likes you, look at the direction of the feet—they'll tell you the truth.

A good sense of direction isn't our legs' only skill. There are many other ways these limbs send out signals. For example, to give a relaxed vibe, try the following:

When sitting:

- Hang your legs so they gently touch the floor.
- Cross your legs at your ankles.
- Cross one leg over your knee.
- Gently tap your foot or rock your leg in time with the music.

When standing:

- Keep your legs slightly apart, in a natural stance (not too tightly together like an army recruit, or too far apart like football player ready for tackle).
- Lean your heel against the ankle of your other foot (but don't wrap your legs around one another).
- Gently tap your foot or move your leg in time with the music.

MOVE SIX

PRACTICE THE ART OF THE FLIRTATIOUS TOUCH

Touching can be your one-way ticket to flirting paradise—or flirting misery. When it comes to this flirting move, remember that less is so much better than more.

A gentle, appropriate touch can generate instant rapport and connection. It can soothe and melt away flirting jitters. It is a crystal clear sign of attraction and interest.

Too much touching, touching too soon, or touching the wrong body parts, however, will instantly turn off your flirting interest. Once that happens, it is virtually impossible to restart the flirting dance, especially if the woman feels threatened. If a man's touch comes off as creepy, the woman will do anything to get away as quickly as possible. Both men and women need to respect their flirting interests' boundaries.

Pay close attention to the reaction when you casually—accidentally or purposely—touch your flirting interest. If you sense any tension or zero reciprocation, back off. It's likely time to move on.

BEFORE YOU TOUCH, ASSESS THE SITUATION

Before you decide to use a flirtatious touch, look for signs that you have permission. Examples include your interest doing any of the following:

- Moving closer to you
- Blocking out the rest of the world to listen to you
- Leaning over to tell you something in your ear or in close range
- Placing their hands close enough to touch yours
- "Accidentally" bumping your arm when walking

Once you get the go-ahead touch vibe, don't be afraid to make your move. If you think about it for too long, it will feel unnatural. Be spontaneous and stay in the moment.

Use a touch appropriate to the situation, with a good sense of timing and harmonious eye contact, facial expressions, and words.

FOR WOMEN: A TOUCH TUTORIAL

A woman who touches a man says she feels comfortable with him, wants to get closer, likes him, trusts him, and wants his attention. What sort of touch communicates those feelings? The following actions are completely acceptable for females (and almost always welcome):

- Handshakes
- Touching his hand, wrist, arm, or shoulder
- Touching his foot with your foot
- Admiring and touching his ring or watch
- Giving him a light, playful push
- **Removing a piece of string or lint from his sweater**

Nervous about trying out a forward touch? Try "accidentally" touching him first. It's a great way to test the waters. Here are some suggested moves:

- When handing him a napkin, let your fingers linger next to his for a few milliseconds.
- When walking next to him, let your hand brush against his.
- When he reaches for something, accidentally move your hands in his direction so your hands touch.
- When seated next to each other, let your legs touch momentarily.

FOR MEN: A TOUCH TUTORIAL

A man who touches a woman says he is attracted to her, testing the romantic waters, and letting others know about his interest. The following are acceptable moves for males:

- Handshakes
- Touching her hand, arm, wrist, or shoulder
- Placing your hand on her lower back to give her the right of way
- Touching her foot with your foot
- Complimenting her and quickly touching her watch, bracelet, or ring

Instead of diving right in, however, consider testing the touching waters first, with one of these "accidental" moves:

- **Brush against her accidentally and watch her reaction.**
- Grasp her hand gently and admire her nails or hands.
- While walking, hold her hand for a few seconds and then let it go.
- When seated next to each other, let your foot or leg briefly touch her foot or leg.

SO YOU'VE TOUCHED. NOW WHAT?

After you've tried a touch, casually watch for a reaction. If there's a smile, a relaxed acceptance of your touch, or reciprocation, you've hit the jackpot. Those are sure signs that s/he likes you. Remember, however, this doesn't give you the green light to keep touching. Continue the flirting dance by keeping the conversation flowing. If after ten minutes or so you feel like another touch could add to the conversation, go for it.

If you get a startled reaction to your touch, back off for the moment. Try making your flirting interest comfortable again by backing up a little and continuing with a lighthearted conversation.

Finally, if you get an extreme reaction—s/he clams up, backs off, or looks scared or angry—it may be time to take your flirting elsewhere. Save your subtle touch for someone who will appreciate it.

FLIRTING TIP: TOUCH WITH CAUTION

Keep it playful, light, nonthreatening, quick, and innocent. Always watch for a reaction and back off if you get an uncomfortable vibe.

A FINAL WORD OF CAUTION: TOUCHING NO-NOS

When you first meet someone, avoid the following moves. Your flirting interest may read them as intrusive, sexual, or inappropriate. (Most of these are obvious, but they're still worth a mention.)

Do not do any of the following:

- Pinch the cheek
- Caress the face
- Touch the leg above the knee
- Touch the tush, breasts, or genitals

WHAT ABOUT HUGGING?

As long as it is playful and appropriate to the situation, hugging is fine. If someone tells you it is his/her birthday or is out celebrating a big promotion, for instance, offer a birthday or congratulatory hug.

To make sure the other person is okay with you giving them a hug, you may first want to say something like "Oh wow, today is your birthday?! You deserve a hug!" and watch for their reaction. If s/he gives you a big a smile in response or says something like "Aww, that is so nice of you, thanks!," take it as a sign that your hug is welcome. If, however, s/he responds by leaning or backing away, or giving you an uncomfortable, worried look, you may want to put the hug on hold. An unwanted hug is never a good thing.

If signs are indeed clear that a hug is welcome, lean in and embrace for just a few seconds—leaving just enough time to give a quick pat to the other person's back. In most cases, the male's arms will naturally go above the females, with her arms softly wrapped around his chest and his arms around her shoulders, but don't worry too much about this. More than anything else, hugs should simply be natural.

As you come out of the embrace, give a smile and continue with your conversation. Chances are, it'll only improve from here on out!

FROM THE FLIRTING FIELD

Steve, fifty, and MaryLou, forty-eight, initially met online, then later in person at a coffee shop. They both arrived at the same time, and when Steve opened the door, he placed his hand on the small of MaryLou's back as she walked through the door. MaryLou said this move was a warm gesture on Steve's part, and it relaxed her.

MOVE SEVEN

LEARN WHAT MEN DO WHEN THEY WANT TO ATTRACT A WOMAN

Have you ever wondered whether men send "I want to meet you" or "I'm attracted to you" signals? The answer to that is yes, they most certainly do.

When a man is interested, he will exhibit a variety of physical signals, from checking his appearance to standing tall and puffing out his chest. (Coincidentally, it is a fact that in some bird species, the male prances around the female while fluffing up his feathers and displaying elaborate body movements so that he can get noticed.) So if your guy struts his stuff in front of you, you have hit the jackpot! Go for it—his actions are his subconscious way of telling you that he likes you.

To get a better understanding of what men do to attract women, try being an "eyewitness" to men who are flirting with women (other than yourself). Casually observe couples and pay attention to what the man is doing and what the woman's reaction is. Take a mental note of what works, what doesn't, and what seems to be the most popular. The quicker you learn to identify these signals, the quicker you will be able to flirt back in your own situations.

LADIES' QUIZ: HOW SIGNAL-SAVVY ARE YOU?

With this little quiz, test your intuition and knowledge of how a man attracts a woman.

1. Which of the following is a sure sign he wants to meet you?
   a. He covers his mouth.
   b. He smoothes or straightens his tie.
   c. He slaps his knee.
   d. He clenches his hands.

2. What is the most common male flirting signal?
   a. Preening (putting the finishing touches on appearance, such as straightening or adjusting clothing)
   b. Buying her a drink
   c. Trying to impress her
   d. Showing disinterest

3. When a man is attracted to a woman across the room, what does he do?
   a. Puts his hands on his hips
   b. Waits for her to come to him
   c. Does nothing
   d. Asks his friend to approach her

4. Which of the following would a man *never* do to express interest in a woman?
   a. Adjust his socks
   b. Show chivalry
   c. Loop his thumbs under his belt
   d. Look at his watch

5. Which of the following is a male signal to attract a woman?
   a. Hands on hips
   b. Feet slightly apart
   c. Raised eyebrows
   d. All of the above

How did you do? The answers are: 1. b, 2. a, 3. a, 4. d, 5. d.

If you got five correct: You have uncanny radar to know when he's interested.

If you got four correct: You really know how to read a man.

If you got three correct: You need to brush up on male flirting signals.

If you got one or two correct: You're missing the signs! You need a full lesson.

If you got none correct: Not to worry, we'll turn you from clueless to savvy in no time. Read on.

SEVEN SIGNALS THAT SAY HE'S INTERESTED

No matter how you did on the quiz, you should know *all* the signals that say he's interested. Flirting happens before either party speaks even a single word, which means spotting the nonverbal signals puts you one step ahead of him!

    The more you notice, the more confident you'll feel and the better you'll flirt because you'll know he wants you to flirt with him. It doesn't get easier than that!

Signal #1: Preening

Men preen—put the finishing touches on their appearance—instinctively. If you asked your favorite guy friend whether he preens, he would say, "No way," but see for yourself. The next time you attend a singles event, check out what guys do when surrounded by many possible dates.

Signs of a guy's preening/interest include the following:

- Fixing his hair
- Straightening or rearranging his tie
- Adjusting his shirt collar
- Removing imaginary lint from his shirt or jacket
- Tucking in or smoothing his shirt
- Tying or retying his shoelaces or pulling up his socks

The preening man tells you he wants to look his best so you will pay attention to him. Because men have no clue that they do this—it's like a subconscious sign of interest—you may want to take this opportunity to make the first move. Compliment his great haircut, his superb taste in clothing, his stylish shoes, his perfectly ironed shirt, his trendy belt, or his classy tie. He will be so happy that you noticed him.

KEEP YOUR EYES PEELED

Ladies, be on the lookout for the preening man. His actions are a dead giveaway that he wants to meet you. And when you do see a sign, take it as an ego boost and make the first move. The ball's in your court!

Signal #2: The Eyebrow Raise

When a man raises his eyebrows, a light bulb has just gone off in his head that says, "I like you. Please come over." He has no control over this, an instinctual male move. If a man raises an eyebrow in your presence, smile to yourself and say, "Yeah, this guy's got his eye on me."

Signal #3: Hands on Hips

When a man stands with his hands on his hips, he's showing you his readiness to meet, sending you a message that says, "I'm waiting for you."

When you see this, walk over to him and with a big smile, say hi. Watch what he does with his hands; once he feels confident you will stick around for the long haul, his hands will relax by his side.

Signal #4: Thumbs in Belt or Hands in Pockets

The flirting guy typically puts his thumbs in his belt hooks or a few fingers in his pockets. This actually sends you two messages—one, that he notices you, and two, that he wants you to approach. This subtle signal often goes unnoticed, so watch for it. The guy acts as manly as possible, hoping that you will give him the time of day.

Signal #5: "Macho" Male

Have you ever noticed a man who, without warning, pulls in his stomach in, pushes his chest forward slightly, and stands up straighter?

This is what we flirty flirts call the "courtship stance." He is sprucing himself up for you! He wants to portray himself as strong, manly, and desirable. He believes that women are attracted to a "hunk" and he is trying his best to be what he thinks would be attractive to a woman. By projecting this positive self image, he wants you to take notice of his manliness.

This man is ready to meet you and is doing everything to muster up strength to make his approach. Give him a break. Say hi. He will appreciate the gesture.

Signal #6: Chivalry

This male flirting signal tells you he thinks you are worth it. Look out for the following signs that chivalry's alive and well. Your man may do one of the following:

- Offer you his seat
- Give you his jacket because you look cold
- Open the door for you
- Let you get ahead of him in line
- Offer to pump your gas

If you are the fortunate beneficiary of chivalry, admire and applaud this gentleman! You won't be disappointed.

Signal #7: The Eighteen-Inch Stance

When a man plants his legs about eighteen inches (46 cm) apart, take it as a great sign. He is marking his territory and saying "This is my space," "Check me out," and "Come on over." This is similar to the animal kingdom, where the male's positioning often sends a message to his rivals to take a hike and simultaneously sends a message to the females that he wants to be recognized.

If you see this stance being displayed, don't be afraid to toss a smile in his direction, or even a hello. He's not trying to intimidate you, just the other guys in the room!

FROM THE FLIRTING FIELD

Betsy, forty-two, was meeting some friends for dinner. While waiting for them, she sat down and started reading a book. When she glanced up, she saw this guy with a great smile sitting across from her. He was fixing his shirt and smoothing his hair. Betsy noticed but did not know what to make of it. She continued reading. When she glanced over again, he was standing up with his chest out and his thumbs in his belt, smiling and looking in her direction.

Betsy got up and walked toward him, said hello, and introduced herself. Dillon, forty-five, offered her a drink and told her he was so happy she came over to him because he wanted to approach her but did not know what to say. Betsy giggled and told him all the flirting signals he gave off. Dillon blushed and said he had no idea, but that he felt as if he had won the lotto! When Betsy's friends arrived, Dillon asked for her number. Six years later, Dillon and Betsy still laugh about Dillon, the master preener. To this day, he still denies it.

MOVE EIGHT

LEARN WHAT WOMEN DO WHEN THEY WANT TO ATTRACT A MAN

Women are more subtle than men when it comes to what they do to attract men. Their actions are typically a bit more complicated to decode. Men *expect* women to fret over their looks, so when a woman fixes her hair or adjusts her shirt, it can be difficult to know whether she's sending out a flirting signal.

That said, women *do* send out flirting signals—they're just a little harder to spot. I'm here to help. I'll show how to break down the signs as easily as possible and make the perfect matching move. But before we get started, I'd ask you to do the same exercise I asked the ladies to do in the last chapter, and that is to observe men and women who are flirting. Watch them interact and see what the women do to get a positive response from men. Do they laugh emphatically, keep tucking their hair behind their ear, or fidget with their bracelet? These might all be signs!

I know you might be saying, "But I don't want them to think I am spying on them." Not to worry, there are plenty of opportunities to subtly observe flirting in action. Some of my favorites include couples: dining together, standing at a bar, waiting in lines, sitting next to each other at a party, or chatting on the bus or subway. All it takes is a little tuning in of the senses, and you'll be amazed by what you notice.

GUYS' QUIZ: HOW SIGNAL-SAVVY ARE YOU?

Before we dive in, let's see how much you know about how women let men know about attraction. No cheating!

1. How do you know a woman wants to meet you?
   a. She puts her hand on her forehead.
   b. She talks to the bartender.
   c. She tosses her head back knowing that you are looking.
   d. She folds her arms in front of her.

2. What is the most common female flirting signal?
   a. Playing with her hair
   b. Talking to her friends
   c. Playing hard to get
   d. Tapping her finger

3. Which would a woman *never* do to express interest in a man?
   a. Cross and uncross her legs
   b. Dangle her shoe
   c. Look bored and annoyed
   d. Expose her wrists

4. What does a woman most commonly do when attracted to a man across the room?
   a. Primp and preen
   b. Sit quietly
   c. Walk in the opposite direction
   d. Talk to her friends to avoid embarrassment

5. Which of the following is a female signal to attract a man?
   a. Hiking up her skirt
   b. Playing with her bracelets and exposing her palms
   c. Adjusting her clothing
   d. All of the above

How did you do? Here are the answers: 1. c, 2. a, 3. c, 4. a, 5. d.

If you got five correct: You are an expert in identifying when a woman wants to meet you.

If you got four correct: You are a connoisseur of knowing when a woman shows interest.

If you got three correct: You are on the right track to knowing when a woman is giving you the green light.

If you got one or two correct: You need help figuring out when she's into you.

If you got none correct: You need to become more signal savvy. Read on!

SEVEN SIGNALS THAT SAY SHE'S INTERESTED

Are you a man both captivated and confused when it comes to deciphering women's flirting signals? Are you sometimes unsure that she's really attracted to you? Do you wonder whether she intends the signals for you or the guy next to you?

The best way to gauge interest is to know which signals females most often give off when they want to catch your eye. If you receive one or more of these signs, it's important to flirt back as quickly and as naturally as you can. If you're the intended recipient, the flirting competition will flourish. (Even if it wasn't meant for you, you never know where it may lead.)

Signal #1: Hair Play

Women love to play with their hair. If you see her run her fingers through her hair, fluff up her hair, or arrange it so it looks perfect, take notice. If she does this while she thinks you are checking her out, approach and tell her what perfect hair she has (or start any sort of conversation, really). In all likelihood, she'll enjoy that you made a move.

Signal #2: Head Toss

You've definitely seen the head toss, when a woman flings her hair back as she raises her head. It's all about getting you to pay attention to her. A woman's hair is her most valuable accessory. So when she tosses it, you should catch it. (Ok, kidding, but do approach her!)

Signal #3: Leg Cross/Uncross

The flirting language of delicately and slowly crossing and uncrossing legs speaks for itself. The woman wants to draw your attention to her. What a perfect time to tell her that you find her skirt attractive! She'll get the real message.

Signal #4: Exposed Wrists

A woman's wrists are a sensual body part. A woman who gently pushes up her sleeves (if she has any) and plays with her watch or bracelet wants you to know that she is open to you. Don't miss the opportunity to ask her for the time.

"IF YOU RECEIVE ONE OR MORE OF THESE SIGNS, IT'S IMPORTANT TO FLIRT BACK AS QUICKLY AND AS NATURALLY AS YOU CAN."

Signal #5: Skirt Hike

While sitting down, the flirtatious woman may raise her skirt just enough to expose her knees—hoping that you'll understand her attraction to you. This subtle sign is sometimes done in combination with the shoe dangle (so don't worry if you miss it).

Signal #6: Shoe Dangle

The flirting woman dangles her high heels off of her foot while seated on a bar stool or high chair. This draws attention to her legs in a playful way. Often she does this in conjunction with crossing her legs—and may be unaware that she's doing either!

FROM THE FLIRTING FIELD

Linda, an attractive, stylish divorcee in her early forties, had become increasingly frustrated and disappointed at singles events. In several of our coaching sessions, she told me she would go to these events and leave feeling worse than when she arrived.

"No one would talk to me. I felt like there was something wrong with me," she said. "I'd notice other women who, in my opinion, were far less attractive than me enjoying themselves, laughing, and talking up a storm. I just didn't get it."

I asked Linda to describe what she did when she went to one of these events. "Basically nothing," she replied. "I just stand around, trying not to look conspicuous, sometimes with my arms folded hoping that a man will approach me." Linda soon realized that she wasn't sending any flirtatious signals. No signals equals no attention! No signals, nothing happens!

Once Linda realized that flirtatious signals could increase her chances of attracting a man, she tried. "Ask me how many guys have approached me," she told me the following week. "I hope you can count that high!"

Signal #7: Primping and Preening (P and P)

P and P means the woman cares about how she looks—not only for herself, but for you. If she does any P and P while looking at you, it's your lucky day—she's doing it solely for you! This is your cue to approach her and compliment how she looks.

P and P signs are any of the following:

- Reapplying lipstick or perfume
- Rearranging her blouse
- Tucking her hair behind her ear
- Playing with her earrings
- Repositioning her necklace

STELLAR SIGNAL RESPONSES

If she signals by:	Respond by saying:
Playing with her hair	"You have beautiful hair."
Tossing her hair and you're in close range	"Your hair smells so nice."
Crossing and uncrossing her legs	"You have the nicest legs in this place."
Exposing her wrists	"I couldn't help noticing your beautiful watch/ bracelet."
Dangling her shoes	"Those are really pretty shoes."
Wearing perfume	"That's a great scent you're wearing. What is it?"
Repositioning her necklace	"That necklace is so unique. It looks perfect on you."

MOVE NINE

WIN OVER YOUR FLIRTING INTEREST WITH MIRRORING

Mirroring is one of flirting's best-kept secrets. Mirroring your flirting interest will make a connection as bonding as super glue.

What is mirroring? Mimicking whatever your flirting interest does—subtly. Emulate body language, voice volume and tone, gestures, and movements. You reflect back what s/he does but not as a carbon copy. As a result, the other person instantly feels more comfortable around you. Congratulations, you've sparked a connection through body language alone.

Mirroring is always understated, but there's nothing subtle about its results. Read on and I'll tell you all about it.

WHEN IS THE BEST TIME TO MIRROR?

Start mirroring after you have spoken to your flirting interest for ten to fifteen minutes. At that point, you'll feel more relaxed and ready to send out "I'm into you" vibes.

WHY MIRROR?

Mirroring creates an instant bond between flirters. Imagine you with your flirting interest; let's call her Ann. As you lean in toward Ann, she ever so slightly moves a bit closer. A few minutes later, because the music is really loud, you speak into Ann's ear so she can hear you. A minute later she motions you to come closer; she wants to tell you something. How do you feel? Could this girl be a keeper? This is marvelous mirroring in motion!

Mirroring is flattery. You demonstrate to the other person that you are in tune and in sync. Instinctively, we gravitate toward those who behave similarly to us. Therefore, when you naturally mirror your flirting interest, you send out a flare that says you feel an attraction.

So if your flirting interest jokes, your mirroring action is to joke back. If s/he moves to the music, sway to the music as well. If it's about the conversation, focus on the flirtee's every word as well. You get the picture.

FLIRTING TIP: MIRROR WITH FRIENDS

Practice mirroring with a friend of the opposite sex. First, mirror his/her behavior for about ten minutes. Then reverse the roles. Pick a juicy, interesting, or emotional topic about which to talk.

HOW TO MIRROR YOUR FLIRTING INTEREST

First, pay attention to your flirting interest's behavior. Note posture, tone of voice, gestures, eye contact, leg and arm position, and so on.

Then, mimic—just be sure to wait thirty to sixty seconds before repeating. For example, if your flirt interest:

- Leans in toward you, lean in
- Takes a sip, take a sip
- Speaks softer or more slowly, speak at a similar pace and in a similar tone
- Touches your arm, touch his/her arm
- Crosses his/her legs, cross your legs
- Smiles at you, smile back
- Holds a gaze for a few seconds, gaze back

Conduct mirroring moves delicately and slowly. If too abrupt, mirroring could appear as mockery or copy cat behavior. This will likely make the other person feel uneasy and self-conscious and be counterproductive to your flirting mission. The more natural your mirroring, the better the results will be. The best mirroring happens when you feel so in tune that *not* mirroring feels strange.

FROM THE FLIRTING FIELD

Don and Lisa, both in their forties, met at happy hour one Friday afternoon. Don was sitting at the bar and Lisa walked over with a cane. Don asked her whether she'd like to sit down and she accepted. At first, Lisa wasn't sure whether Don really wanted her there or whether he was simply being polite. They began chatting and next thing she knew, two hours had passed.

In our coaching session, Lisa mentioned that when she touched Don's arm, he reciprocated. When she adjusted her chair, he adjusted his. "It was as if he was saying, 'I really like you.'" Lisa said. "I had no idea then that mirroring was happening. It just felt that we were

THE TOP TEN FLIRTING TIPS OF ALL TIME

You have reached the halfway mark of your flirting marathon! You are well on your way to becoming a top-notch flirt. I have confidence in you.

My top ten list of flirting tips contains the most important flirting facts to remember. They will assist you when you need a flirting pep talk and act as a great reference to refer back to after you finish the book.

The most skillful and experienced flirts utilize at least six of these tips in every flirting encounter. What about you? Make flirting happen.

TIP #10: FLIRT WITH THE RIGHT ATTITUDE

A great flirt is self-confident and not afraid to take risks. Be enthusiastic and positive.

TIP #9: START A CONVERSATION

The best opening line is "Hello!" Talk about the surroundings, ask a question, ask for help, or state an opinion.

TIP #8: HAVE FUN

Be playful, lighthearted, and spontaneous. Let your sense of humor—or whatever is special about you—shine through.

TIP #7: USE PROPS

Never leave home without a prop. Props encourage conversation and compel others to start talking to you. Amazing props include pets, unusual jewelry, a fabulous scent, a school sweatshirt, an eye-catching tie, or an interesting book or magazine. (For more about props, see page 184.)

TIP #6: BE THE HOST

Change your behavior from guest to host. Instead of remaining the passive person in waiting, take charge of the welcoming committee.

TIP #5: MAKE THE FIRST MOVE

Move closer, pay a compliment, make eye contact, or say hi to the person you want to meet.

TIP #4: LISTEN

You have two ears and only one mouth because you should listen twice as much as you should talk. Practice active listening. You will draw in your flirting partner, and you will immediately feel important.

TIP #3: MAKE EYE CONTACT

Make direct eye contact but make sure that you look your flirting interest in the eye *gently* and with ease. No deep stares or intense gazing—they're turn-offs.

TIP #2: COMPLIMENT

Compliment your flirting partner. It lets him/her know that you really noticed the details. Just be sure to speak honestly, sincerely, and genuinely. It will take you far!

TIP #1: SMILE

It's contagious! Smiling will make you much more approachable. A smile lights up your face and draws people to you. You will be a people magnet. Try it!

PART TWO

In Part One, we talked about how your amazing body communicates without words, just like the beautiful instrument it is. Now it's time to set some words to the music!

You must sync your words and your actions to be a superb flirt. In this section, you will learn how to combine the techniques from Part One—eye contact, perfect distance, smile, touch, mirroring, the flirtatious handshake, and so on—with verbal strategies to wow even the unwowable.

As I describe actions such as how to work a room, make small talk, deliver great opening lines, practice listening, and use flirting props, imagine yourself fulfilling my suggestions. Envision yourself using these techniques. You can even practice out loud as you are reading or in front of the mirror. Visualize yourself working a room and approaching someone. Practice to become a flirting star.

Once you master these techniques, flirting will feel as natural as putting your keys in the ignition, emailing a friend, or brushing your teeth. You will be able to flirt naturally and confidently and show off the real you!

MOVE ONE

WORK THE ROOM TO STAND OUT

Can working a room really make your dreams come true? Simply answer yes or no to the following questions to find out.

1. Would it be wonderful if you knew when and where you would meet the man or woman of your dreams?
2. Would it be your lucky day if the guy or gal you've been eyeing was your date next Saturday?
3. Would it be great if your dream-come-true man or woman was in the same room as you?
4. Would it be a disaster if your dream-come-true man or woman was in the same room as you and you never met him/her?
5. Would it be a disaster if your dream-come-true was the cousin of the person sitting next to you and you never spoke to him/her?

If you answered "yes" to four or more of the questions, read on to learn why working a room will maximize your chances of finding the love you seek.

MAKE IT A HOBBY: SIX STEPS TO BEING A SOCIAL BUTTERFLY

I have never had conventional hobbies. I don't ski, cycle, scuba dive, paint, garden, or bake. I do have one favorite pastime, however: working a room. I come alive at cocktail parties, conferences, awards dinners, networking events, or charity functions. No matter how tired or exhausted I am, put me in a room of strangers and I'm in my glory. I love meeting new people, finding out what makes them tick, what they like, where they live, what they do, who they know, what they enjoy, and so on. I love making strangers feel comfortable, making them laugh, and enjoying the spontaneity and adventure of connecting. I never know who I may meet or how they may enrich my life.

   For most people, working a room is not a favorite pastime. I hope to change that for you. The benefits of working a room can outweigh the discomfort that situation makes you feel. Trust me!

Social Butterfly Step #1: Embrace the Idea

Do any of these scenarios sound familiar?

- Rochelle and Laila, both twenty-nine, always attend a monthly single professionals networking event. The same situation happens each time: They get a drink, find a seat, and spend the whole evening talking to each other. *Rochelle and Laila both know how to work the room, but they feel uncomfortable doing it (and then wonder why they don't meet anyone).*

- Vinny, thirty-seven, has a successful career and wants to settle down. He regularly attends a Catholic singles event that attracts at least a hundred people each time. He usually talks to the same organizer each week or the volunteer at the registration desk. *Vinny does not know how to work a room and therefore clings to anyone he knows.*

- Theresa, thirty-four, attends a variety of singles events. She typically talks to the first person who approaches and spends the whole evening with that man—whether she likes him or not. It's just easier. *Theresa wants to work the room, but she does not know how to excuse herself gracefully from the nonstop talker.*

What do these individuals share? Like you, they all *want* to put themselves out there and meet new people, but none of them is sure how.

The first step to transition from sidelined to social butterfly lies in changing your mindset. Don't consider "working a room" work. Think of it as enjoying, experiencing, or reaping the benefits of the room. Put a positive spin on it.

Think of events with large groups as ideal places to meet others for fun, friendship, or romance. You have the chance to connect with unending possibilities, so don't miss out.

WHAT EXACTLY IS "WORKING A ROOM"?

To work a room, you check out the attendees by mingling, chatting, socializing, or hitting it off with a few people you really connect with or want to learn more about.

Social Butterfly Step #2: Prepare *Before* You Arrive

Do you think that working a room doesn't start until the party or event begins? Think again! The best social butterflies come prepared, both physically and mentally. Here are some pre-event guidelines from which anyone interested in working a room will benefit:

- Look your best. Be fresh and well-groomed.
- Select an outfit you feel good in and one that will get you noticed (tasteful, of course).
- Leave your baggage at home. This includes your job worries, horror stories about your ex, the fight you had with your boss, or your kid's problems in school.
- Focus on the adventure and excitement of meeting potential dates.
- Have your business cards easily accessible. (We'll talk more about this later.)
- Brush up on the day's newsy items. Read the newspaper, listen to the news, or find the latest happenings online.
- Give yourself a pep talk. Remind yourself that you are going out to meet new people and not just to talk to your friend (just make sure to tell your friend your plan).
- Have an opening line handy. "What brings you here?" is particularly great because it get greats mileage and often leads to establishing a shared interest. ("Oh, you're here to listen to the Bryan Brown Band play? Me too. I love their music...") From there, you can talk about anything—the event, movies, concerts, plays, schools you have attended, favorite restaurants, your occupation, or the dream vacation you'd take if you won the lottery.

"SELECT AN OUTFIT YOU FEEL GOOD IN AND ONE THAT WILL GET YOU NOTICED (TASTEFUL, OF COURSE)."

Social Butterfly Step #3: Rev Up Upon Arrival

For this step, think of yourself as a pilot almost ready to land. You have approached your destination and are preparing for touchdown. Doing the following will ensure a smooth, bump-free landing and will leave you feeling self-assured and on top of your game.

- Check your coat, umbrella, backpack, briefcase, and so on. Don't forget to turn off your cell phone and put away any other electronics. Give others the impression that you actually want to be there and are interested.
- Arrive early and then be part of the welcoming committee. By arriving early, you can get comfy with the place, talk to another early arriver or the host, and prepare for the rest of the event.
- Do a once-over to scope out your prospects and to become familiar with your surroundings. Pay attention to seating and the location of food, drinks, the restrooms, and any other key spots. If you know something about the place, you'll have something to share with your flirting interests.
- Remember why you are at the event. *(Hint: It's to meet new people.)*

Social Butterfly Step #4: Let the Real Fun Begin

The party is rolling and you're ready to start socializing! You look good and feel better. Take one last moment to clear your head and focus on what you know. Let's review for a moment:

- Have good posture.
- Make eye contact.
- Smile.
- Keep an appropriate distance.
- Shake hands.
- Show interest.
- Have fun.

Now it's time to walk the walk and talk the talk. You can do it.

Walk as if you have a destination, but all the time in the world to get there. Don't look like you're running to catch a bus or dragging yourself like you just finished a marathon. Walk around the room like the master of ceremonies, the maître d', the owner, or the guest of honor. Act as if you belong, not like a fish out of water.

Social Butterfly Step #5: Make the First Move

Making the first move is really hard, but failing to do so will harm your love life. If you don't make the first move, someone else will. Start by talking to someone who is alone, looks as nervous as you, looks approachable, or is next to you—just about anyone.

Even though you may have butterflies in your stomach, just getting the words out will help you mitigate the "anxiety minefield" that may have been building up inside. Before you know it, the butterflies will fade and your enjoyment of the moment will increase.

Everything gets easier after that first line. In no time, you'll regain your composure—if you lost it at all—and continue with your conversation. Flirting is a social skill which improves with practice and repetition. The more you do it, the greater your comfort level will be.

Finally, remember that you are there to meet potential dates. If you spend half the evening plotting your first move, before you know it, the place is closing and you still have not spoken to a soul. Get moving!

WHY MAKE THE FIRST MOVE?

Because it does the following:

- Makes the event more interesting
- Empowers you
- Lets others know that you have confidence
- Keeps you from not talking to anyone
- Flatters your flirting interest
- Makes future moves easier
- Increases your chances for flirting success
- Prevents you from having any regrets about not making a move
- Helps reduce the social anxiety of not talking or awkward silence

Social Butterfly Step #6: Be the Host with the Most

This is one of my favorite tips for working the room: Think of yourself as the party's host rather than as a guest. You aren't a passive person waiting but rather the welcoming committee.

You are probably saying to yourself, "I don't like doing that," "I'm not good at it," or "I rarely have any luck." If that's the case, changing your behavior seems like a good idea, right?

Playing host takes the focus off of you and places it on your flirting interest. You have a job to do: make your flirting interest feel good. This change in focus should help you feel less nervous and more in charge. For those who despise mingling, this is a great trick because it allows you to forget about your nerves and focus on your party guests.

Next time you attend a gathering, try these party-hosting techniques:

- Introduce yourself. As I mentioned above, look for individuals who are alone, nearby, or look nervous or approachable. What's most important here, though, is that you simply *start talking*. Don't dwell too much on finding the perfect "potential." You'll meet that person eventually. In the meantime, get your mouth moving!
- Once you start talking to someone, ask the person how s/he is doing, how s/he finds the event, or whether s/he is having fun.
- Ask to get the person a drink, a dessert, or so on.
- Give the person extra space at a crowded event, ("Let me move over a bit to make you more comfortable..."). If you're a man speaking to a woman, offer her a seat.
- Smile frequently.
- Offer to help ("I see you are waiting for a free restroom; there's another less-crowded one down the hall...").
- Make small talk to make the other person feel welcome ("I got so lost trying to find this place. How about you?").

With the conversation started, continue asking questions and getting to know the other person. Remember, you goal is to make him/her feel good—which is often as easy as listening intently or paying compliments.

If others show interest in joining your conversation, invite them in. You increase your odds of finding someone who really interests you with the more people you get to know.

WHAT TO DO WHEN A CONVERSATION GOES SOUTH (OR YOU JUST NEED A BREAK!)

We've all been there: A conversation starts out nice, but a few minutes in, it fizzles. You'd like to get away—whether to go meet other new people or because you simply can't stand it a minute longer. In these situations, use any of the following get-away lines.

For someone you never want to see/talk with again, use one of the following lines:

- "Sorry, I need to go meet my friend."
- "It's late. I've got to get going."
- "I'm going to walk around a bit. Have a good night."
- "I was actually just about to go use the restroom. Take care."
- "Excuse me. I need to take this call." (Pretend your phone is vibrating.)

Keep it short and simple—don't feel you have to offer a lengthy explanation—and do so as soon as you feel like getting away. We often "stick around" because we don't want to hurt the other person's feelings, but in fact, the more you linger, the more you are leading this person on. Cut it quick and physically remove yourself from the situation; head to another room or area, if possible.

FLIRTING Q&A: "SPARKS ARE FLYING (I THINK), BUT HOW DO I KNOW FOR SURE?"

The answer is simple. Ask a subtle question that offers the other person the chance to step away, such as "I'm having such a great time talking to you... I just hope I'm not keeping you from something?"

If s/he says, "Of course not! I'm enjoying myself as well," you've got the green light to continue the convo. Likewise, if the person takes your question as an opportunity to make a hasty retreat, you've got your answer, too—and the chance to move on to people more worthy of your time!

For someone from whom you just want to take a break so you can mingle more, use one
of the following lines:

- "I've really enjoyed talking with you, but I should say hi to a few people before heading
  out. Here's my card. It would be great to get together."
- "I need to make a quick phone call/tell my friend I'm still here/order another drink,
  but I'd love to continue talking. What do you say we meet back here in ten minutes?"
- "I have been having so much fun and would love to continue talking, but I have to
  get going. How about continuing our conversation over dinner next week?"
- "Our friends are probably feeling neglected. Want to try to get our groups to mingle?
  We'll make it a joint effort, and then reconnect in five. Sound good?"

Don't fear breaks. They're a great way for you to stand back, collect your thoughts,
and survey the spark factor. If you were both into each other, there's no doubt you'll
connect again.

THE ART AND SCIENCE OF THE BUSINESS CARD

Let's say you've been talking to someone for at least a half hour. The vibes and body language are positive. All signs point to mutual interest, but you just don't know. For some reason or another, one of you must go. Now's the perfect time to introduce the business card. Simply say, "I'm having a great time with you and would love to get together. Here's my card."

It's easier than requesting a phone number. Someone who shares your interest will surely accept your card and offer one in return (or write down his/her contact information). Someone who doesn't want to stay in touch will likely squirm, stutter, or say or do nothing. When this happens, pack up, smile, and say, "I see someone over there I need to talk with. It was nice meeting you." (If you continue mingling at the same event, try another part of the room.)

IS THERE A RIGHT TIME OR WRONG TIME FOR THE BUSINESS CARD?

Wait at least twenty minutes into a conversation before asking for or offering a card or phone number. Making the request before that says that you want *anybody's* phone number and not specifically the person with whom you're speaking.

Why the Card? And What If I Don't Have One?

Business cards are great for making professional and social connections because of their practicality; they offer a simple way to exchange numbers and information. Flirters without cards are like restaurants without menus.

What if you don't have a card or feel reluctant to give one out because it contains all of your work information? Make a flirting card! It provides your name and the appropriate phone number and email address. Personalize your flirting card by doing one of the following:

- Choosing an unusual color (such as dusty rose or electric blue)
- Selecting an eye-catching, clear font
- Adding something to make it memorable (such as a symbol or picture that relates to you)

Because business cards typically say what you do, a card without that information will spark conversation about your work life. If you feel silly having a card with only your name and contact information, consider adding a line that hints at your profession (for example, "consultant," "editor," "coach," or "sales rep") rather than listing your full title. This may spark even more interest!

Finally, no matter what type of card you have, have it handy!

It ruins the moment if you have to go get it out of your coat pocket or empty out your bulging purse or wallet.

SHOULD I FLY SOLO OR WITH A WINGMAN?

Having support when you work a room can make flirting seem easier. The two of you can walk over to two women or guys and strike up a conversation. It may even seem more natural or fun that way. Conversely, an upbeat, entertaining conversation between you and your pal could invite others to join in (assuming you keep yourselves open to the crowd).

So here's my advice: If flying duo gives you wings to work the room, go for it! If flying duo makes you stick to your friend like glue, solo sailing is the answer for you.

Flirting with a Wingman

If you decide to work a room with a partner, consider the following steps:

- Walk in together.
- Separately, do a once-over of the place.
- Spend ten minutes or so together assessing the situation.
- Make a plan to head your separate flirting ways. Before you part, decide on a check-in time. Your time frame will depend largely on the length of the event; at a two-hour art event, for example, you may meet up after an hour. At a bar or party, it may be after just ten minutes. Whatever the time frame, make the best of the flirting time you have.
- Decide at your check-in what time you will leave the event.
- Enjoy working the room! By night's end, you'll surely have some great stories to share with your friend.

FLIRTING TIP: MAKE A CHEAT SHEET

Worried you may forget one of the steps? Jot them down on the back of one of your flirting cards and do a quick review before you arrive. Know that's "the" card by making it a different color or marking it somehow. It'll be our little secret!

READY, SET, WORK IT!

Now that you have all the tools to work a room, feel confident and ready to get out there (for even more ammo, read the next step to learn some killer opening lines).

Let's review one last time the keys to working a room:

- Prepare yourself to work the room.
- Give the room a once-over before you begin.
- Walk the walk.
- Make the first move.
- Be the host, not a guest.
- Have your flirting card ready—and use it.
- Fly solo or duo: it's up to you.
- Enjoy.

MOVE TWO

MAKE THE FIRST MOVE—GREAT OPENING LINES TO FIND LOVE

Are you a perfect schmoozer or a schmoozer wannabe? A perfect schmoozer can talk about anything with anybody because s/he listens, ask loads of questions, and is truly interested in what the other person has to say.

The perfect schmoozer has the gift of gab, makes small talk a hobby, and speaks in a way that just flows. They also often have a great sense of humor and a playful attitude. Sounds like a great combination, right?

Well, you can be that same type of person! Even if small talk does not come naturally to you, you can change that. Read on and practice what I preach. As the queen of schmoozers, I'll show you how to replace your small talk jitters with self-assurance and ease. With the right tools, we all can be the perfect schmoozer. Are you ready to learn how?

OPENING LINES 101: THE BASICS

Great opening lines fit like a glove. They're like your favorite pair of sweats, softest sweater, most comfortable pair of shoes, or most beat-up jeans. You want to wear them over and over. And you can! When you have a great opening line that works, use and reuse it to your heart's content (as long as you use it on different people).

Want to deliver your own impressive opening line? Let's start with the basics. An opening line is a statement or question that gets the attention of your flirting interest. It can be funny, intriguing, or complimentary (as long as it works). Strong, thoughtful opening lines make a fabulous first impression, break the ice between you and your flirting interest, and help establish a warm connection.

THE BENEFITS OF BEING PREPARED

Just as preparing too much can work against you, so can not being prepared at all. Consider this story and the lessons we can learn from it.

Jeff, a handsome twenty-six-year-old, was waiting for the gym to open. Marissa, an adorable, fit twenty-three-year-old arrived a few minutes later. Jeff immediately thought, "She looks incredible. I better make a move before anyone else comes on the scene." Without thinking, Jeff blurted out, "Did you come here to work out?"

Rolling her eyes, Marissa replied, "Um, yeah, isn't that what gyms are for?" and turned away.

What should Jeff have done? He should have prepared himself with a great opening line, that's what. Any of the following would have been great choices:

- "Hi, the gym is supposed to open at 6 a.m., right?" followed by, "What brings you here so early?"
- "At least we won't have to fight for a treadmill, right?" followed by, "Do you typically come here in the mornings?"
- "Hi, I'm Jeff. I'm supposed to be going to the spinning class today—it's my first time. Are you also going?"

To deliver the best opening lines, however, you must remove any possible mental obstacles. In my experience, these obstacles happen for three reasons: worrying too much, clamming up, and feeling embarrassed. We need to let all of that go.

OPENING LINE STUMBLING BLOCKS: THEY'RE ALL IN YOUR HEAD

People sometimes obsess over crafting the "ultimate" opening line and waste more time thinking about it than actually saying something. If you find yourself in this dilemma, remember that any opening line, by its nature, carries with it inherent risk; but even a bad one can be saved (we'll get to that later). You just have to try. There are thousands of great opening lines; just pick one and use it. When worrying starts to overcome your thoughts, remind yourself that nothing ventured is nothing gained!

I call the second obstacle the *flirting freeze moment*, when instead of making the first move, we clam up and go mute. This is especially common with flirting interests to whom we feel highly attracted—as the stakes increase, our anxiety and reluctance rise as well (go figure!). Get out of the deep freeze by facing your fear. Just start talking! I promise the jitters will fade as your conversation takes off.

Lastly, we have all worried about embarrassment over not getting the exact response we want. But won't you be more embarrassed if you do nothing? Remind yourself that a person really worth your time will greet your line with kindness.

WHAT MAKES AN OPENING LINE GREAT?

In my experience, the best opening lines are one or more of the following:

- Spontaneous
- Fun
- Lighthearted
- Witty
- Sincere
- Playful
- Honest
- Open-ended (i.e., a question)
- Positive
- Complimentary
- Genuine
- Confident
- Slightly mysterious
- Reflective of who you are

THE BEST STRATEGIES FOR DELIVERING OPENING LINES THAT WORK

Rather than listing hundreds of opening lines for you to memorize, I want to give you a variety of strategies to use to create your own unparalleled, out-of-the-ordinary opening lines. Once you learn the strategies, it will be a piece of cake to adapt your opening lines to any situation. (A skilled flirter can successfully employ more than one strategy at a time, so feel free to mix and match.)

Strategy #1: Keep It Simple, Just Say "Hi"

My flirting students always ask, "What is *the* best opening line? I never know what to say." For beginners or those intimidated by the thought of approaching another person, I say this: Don't sweat it!

By far, the best opening line is an energetic, confident, animated "hi" or "hello." Why is it so effective? Because it is simple, direct, and honest. You don't have to worry—especially if you have the flirting jitters (which we all get)—about making a long opener. You just have to utter a single, simple word. Team that word with warm eye contact, a big smile, and a quick introduction, and who can resist? (When you're feeling ready to make your next move, head to strategy #2.)

FLIRTING TIP: DON'T BE SHY WITH YOUR HELLOS

Try saying hi to strangers in the supermarket, the fast food line, the dental office waiting room, a bookstore, the airport—anywhere. Think of it as your daily flirting exercise. Practicing daily will make it that much easier to say hi to Mr. or Ms. Fabulous.

Strategy #2: Pay a Compliment

Compliments make great opening lines because everyone loves to be noticed and told something affirming. It makes people feel special and secure.

From my arsenal of opening-line strategies, using compliments is my all-time favorite. It is the most natural way to start a conversation, and it always generates pleasurable results. Complimenting someone also continues a conversation. It sets a positive, upbeat tone. Think about how you feel when a stranger takes the time to compliment you. When I receive a compliment from a stranger, I beam from ear to ear. It's instant happiness.

What elements make up a great compliment? First and foremost, it is honest, genuine, and sincere. Your flirting interest will see right through one that's not and feel awkward, uncomfortable, and embarrassed. If you can't find something about which to compliment someone, move on to another strategy (or another person).

Second, exceptional compliments have the element of surprise and are specific. The surprise factor heightens the compliment's effect exponentially. Imagine that you have received the same compliment a million times: that you look like an actor/actress or sports figure or that you have big eyes or great hair. Hearing the same compliments is nice—but nothing special. Then you receive an unexpected compliment or one that tells you your flirting interest pays attention. It makes you perk up.

Here are some examples of exceptional compliments:

- To a guy in shorts: *"Great legs...are you a triathlete?"*
- To a stunning woman you hear speaking: *"You have a great voice... are you in radio?"*
- To an attractive guy standing in line next to you: *"I am so impressed by the fact that you seem so calm even though we've been waiting for forty-five minutes."*
- To a woman standing in a bar: *"Your shoes are so perfect for your outfit."*
- To a man talking to his friend: *"I couldn't help overhearing your conversation; you sound like such a cooking expert—and I could seriously use some tips."*

FROM THE FLIRTING FIELD

Barbara, thirty-six, one of my former seminar attendees, sat next to Todd at a conference. After one look at him, her cheeks flushed, her heart fluttered, her stomach gurgled, and a voice in her head said, "Give him a compliment." (I taught her well!) All Barbara could think of was how his shoes were so perfectly polished. So she gulped and said, "Your shoes are shined so nicely. Do you get them professionally done?"

Todd smiled and said, "Yes, at least once a week, sometimes more often. I can't believe that you noticed my shoes. I'm actually really flattered because sometimes I think it is a bit extravagant, but it certainly paid off now—I may not have met you otherwise!"

Strategy #3: Once You Learn a Name, Use It

Don't you love when a person uses your name? Don't you hate it when your name is Elizabeth and someone calls you Betty, you're a Maria and you get called Marie, or your name is Tim and someone calls you Tom? It's crucial to get names right. When you use a person's name in a conversation, their ears perk up and their interest in you grows.

The quickest and easiest way to use a person's name is upon introduction. When introduced, immediately say, "It's so good to meet you, [*insert name*]." Repeating it right away will help you remember the name and context for the meeting and communicate to the other person that you were listening.

After your initial use, incorporate the name into the conversation a few more times using lines similar to the following:

- "Fran, can I get you anything?"
- "Fran, is that short for Francesca?"
- "Fran, do you have a pen I may use?"

Focusing on a person's name also provides a great springboard for some interesting conversation. Ask about the story or meaning behind a person's name, whether s/he has any nicknames, or what his/her middle name is.

FLIRTING TIP: FORGOT A NAME? GET IT BACK!

If you can't remember a person's name, the best way to get it back is to be honest and say, "I can't believe that I forgot your name," or "My mind just went blank," or "Your name has completely escaped me." Although it may seem embarrassing, it really can work to your advantage. You show your human imperfections, which make you real and more approachable.

As a last resort, ask the person how to spell his/her name. If the response is something simple such as J-O-E or J-I-L-L, your only way out is to come clean and say, "I guess I should have just asked you to tell me your name again." Hopefully, this faux pas will be an icebreaker, not a deal breaker.

Strategy #4: Use Your Surroundings as a Conversation Starter

Imagine you're at a wedding, waiting in line, on the train, perusing a bookstore, or doing just about anything. You see someone who catches your eye. You want to say something. You really want to meet that person. But you get nervous and still don't know what to say. You need to come up with something—fast!

Look around you. Your surroundings will give you so many conversation topics. Think about what you see, what you hear, what you notice, or what you smell.

Check out anything and everything around you, from the carpet's color to the coffee's aroma to the way the bartender mixes the drink to the excitement you feel about seeing the concert that's about to start. Then comment about it. Talk or state an opinion about the people, food, décor, host, bride, wait, price of gas, item in the store you can't find, adorable child—anything!

Think of your surroundings as your flirting first aid rescue. Use them to stay in the moment and connect with your flirting interest. After all, you already have something in common—you are waiting in line together, taking the same class, or guests at the same party. Use that to your advantage.

WHAT A GREAT OPENING LINE IS *NOT*

Opening lines should not be any of the following:
- Insulting: "I like your hair—except for the color of the roots."
- Condescending: "That jacket looks so worn out. Did you get it from a second-hand store?"
- Negative: "You look miserable. What's wrong?"
- Sexual: "I've never seen such amazing cleavage."
- Overly personal or related to money, income, age, weight, personal issues, and so on: "Can I ask how old you are? My friends and I were trying to guess."
- Overused or tacky: "Hey pretty lady. Come here often?"
- Rhetorical: "Did you come here for dinner?" (asked at a restaurant)

SUPER STARTER STATEMENTS

Use your surroundings to your advantage with these simple lines:

- **At a restaurant:** "How long have you been here? You seem so relaxed even though it looks like the wait is about an hour." or "These appetizers are so interesting. I wonder what this one is."
- **At a bar:** "These watermelon martinis are the best!"
- **At a bookstore:** "I'm new to this store; any idea where I might find the nonfiction section?"
- **At an electronics store:** "There are so many laptops to choose from, it's a bit overwhelming."
- **At a wedding:** "The bride and groom look like they stepped straight out of a magazine."
- **Anywhere:** "This room is freezing. Am I the only one who's cold?"

FROM THE FLIRTING FIELD

Rozzie, thirty-seven, a former client, was in a store looking for a laptop. Not knowing that there would be dozens from which to choose, she quietly said, "I can't believe how many laptops there are here."

The woman next to her agreed and said her brother, who was in the next aisle, was a computer expert and would be back in a minute. When Joey returned, his sister asked him to could give Rozzie some help.

Joey, forty, was happy to oblige and gave Rozzie some great tips. In the end, she was able to select a laptop she loved and was so appreciative that she told Joey she was the luckiest shopper to have met him. Joey and his sister were about to grab lunch, so he asked Rozzie to join them. The two hit it off at lunch and exchanged phone numbers before dessert

Strategy #5: Ask Phenomenal Questions

What can you do if you feel shy or unsure of yourself but don't want to miss out on a flirting op? Ask a flirtatious question!

What is a flirtatious question? It's upbeat and positive, intriguing and complimentary, gets the other person talking, and can be answered with more than a "yes" or a "no."

Why ask flirtatious questions? They jumpstart the conversation and determine whether the initial attraction lives on. Getting an answer to your question is a bonus!

FLIRTING TIP: ASK ANYWAY!

Ask for help even if you don't need it. It's a natural way to start talking to your flirting interest. Don't worry, s/he will never know!

QUESTIONS GALORE

From starters to silly ones, questions can make your flirting talk exciting and interesting. I have outlined some examples for you below, and I encourage you to use them as a guide. Try coming up with some of your own, with charm and personality to make them reflect you.

Type of Question	Sample Questions
Starter questions: Like scrumptious appetizers, these create a great beginning that may lead to a main course or even dessert! A starter question that takes off will lead to an awesome conversation.	• At a social gathering: "Hi, I'm Josh's cousin. Who do you know here?" or "Who did you come with?" • At a seminar: "What do you think of the lecture so far?" • In the produce section of a grocery store: "Do you know how to pick a ripe cantaloupe?" • In the bookstore: "I'm buying my friend a book about rock 'n roll. Any suggestions?" • In a hotel lobby: "You have a great accent. Where are you from?" • In a bar: "That looks interesting. May I ask what you're drinking?"
Personal questions: As the name suggests, these dig deeper. We all love to talk about ourselves, so fire away with questions will that get your flirting interest talking!	• "What's your favorite...[ice cream/food perfume/book]?" • "What do you think of...[particular sports team/news topic/car type]?" • "What would you do if you...[met the person of your dreams/found $100/got a great job in another state]?" • "What are you most passionate about... [hobbies/work/family stuff]?"
Silly questions: Amusing, humorous, or comical questions get the other person laughing, break the ice, and ease the nerves.	• Are you superstitious about anything? • Have you ever gone to work wearing two different shoes? • How are your socks arranged in your drawer?

Type of Question	Sample Questions
Unusual questions: Out of the ordinary, inquisitive questions lend themselves to interesting dialog and thought-provoking conversation.	• "What is the funniest or most interesting item in your pocket or pocketbook?" • "How did you get your name?" • "What makes you laugh?" • "I love jokes; do you know any?"
Relationship-status questions: These questions find out whether your flirting interest is married or taken, without being overly obvious.	• "Did your girlfriend/boyfriend buy you that necklace?" • "What does your husband/wife do?" • "Does your girlfriend/boyfriend like [whatever you are doing...watching sports/drinking coffee/playing tennis] as much as you do?" • "Did your wife match that tie to that shirt?" • "Should I try to guess how long you've been married?"
Help questions: These questions ask for someone's help and show that you value his/her knowledge or skill, even if you do not know this person well. Your flirting interest will be impressed. Once you get the help you need, follow it up with a thank you, compliment, or an offer to return the favor!	• At a bar: "Could you help me get the bartener's attention?" • At a store: "I've never made salmon before; do you know how to cook it? • At a class (or after): "I didn't catch what the instructor said. Would you mind explaining it to me?" • At the gas station: "Could you help me figure out how to use this gas pump? I've never seen this type before."

Strategy #6: Say "Goodbye" Instead of "Hello"

I know this sounds like a contradiction, but sometimes the best opening line is saying "goodbye." This can work if:

- You've spent the whole evening building up your courage to say hi but never did.
- Your flirting interest arrived, and you were leaving.
- You didn't approach him/her, and now the party is over.

In these situations, say, "Hi. I was on my way out, but I didn't want to leave without introducing myself. I'm Josh." You may delay your departure if your goodbye is a success! At places you frequent such as the gym, coffee shop, supermarket, post office, or bank, you could just say, "Bye! Have a good weekend," and when you see the person next, say, "Good to see you again" followed by a compliment or question.

TRANSFORM YOUR QUESTION FROM DULL TO DYNAMIC

Have you ever asked someone a question to break the ice and as soon as you said it knew that it was really mind-numbing? Even if you asked a boring question, turn it around by acting quickly. Make your response to your flirting interest's answer fun and playful. Here are few examples:

Question: "Do you know what time this bar closes?"
Answer: "Midnight."
Your response: "Excellent. That means I have at least another hour to get to know you."

Question: "Do you know where the restrooms are?"
Answer: "Over there."
Your answer: "Good to know. But I didn't really want to know; I actually just wanted an excuse to introduce myself to you."

THE FINAL QUIZ: TEST YOUR OPENING LINE IQ

Let's make sure you're ready to make the first move in style. Read each of the following opening lines and answer "yes" if you think it's a good pick-up line or "no" if you think it should be dumped.

1. "Your outfit looks really expensive. It must have cost you a whole paycheck."
2. "I overheard you two having a heated argument. Do you mind if I join you?"
3. "The design on your shirt is so unique."
4. "Do you mind if I join your group? You seem to be having a great time."
5. "You look much older than the crowd here. Do you come here often?"

Read on to see how you did and why some of these lines are duds and some are definite dos.

Answer #1: No

Although you appear to offer a compliment, money talk is an absolute no-no, and how much someone earns is none of your business.

Answer #2: No

It's inappropriate to point out something personal or negative taking place and then to ask to be a part of it. Mind your manners!

Answer #3: Yes

This is a compliment that says you have been eyeing the other person and that you noticed a detail about his/her appearance. It's also great because you can follow it up with discussion about where or how to get similar clothing or favorite shopping spots.

Answer #4: Yes

This is absolutely correct! This time, you are pointing out something positive and asking whether it's okay for you to join.

Answer #5: No

This is not a compliment; it's a put down and way too personal. It will make your flirting interest—and probably you, too—feel uncomfortable. Stay away from age talk in general.

YOU'VE GOT THE TOOLS—NOW MAKE IT HAPPEN!

Need a quick refresher before you hit the road? No problem! Here is a quick recap of all the opening line strategies you now have in your arsenal:

- Strategy #1: Keep it simple and just say hi.
- Strategy #2: Pay a compliment.
- Strategy #3: Once you learn a name, use it.
- Strategy #4: Use your surroundings as a conversation starter.
- Strategy #5: Ask phenomenal questions.
- Strategy #6: Say goodbye instead of hello.

Now that you have what it takes to be the perfect schmoozer, test your skills. You'll be so glad you did.

FROM THE FLIRTING FIELD

Kristen, forty, a former seminar attendee, and her sister Michele, thirty-two, were volunteering with a singles organization building a house for a family in need.

All afternoon, Kristen kept saying to Michele that she wanted to meet the foreman, Mike, but she never had the opportunity to strike up a conversation. When they were about to leave, Kristen saw Mike and said, "I never had a chance to meet you, so I thought I would give you my business card before I left. It would be nice to touch base sometime."

Smiling, Mike said, "Sure, here's my card too." Kristen couldn't believe she had the confidence to do that. And taking the risk paid off—a week later Mike called and they went out for dinner.

MOVE THREE

LISTEN TO MAKE YOU A PEOPLE MAGNET

Until now we have focused on the *actions* you need to take to be a natural flirt. We have gone over the importance of good eye contact, a warm smile, and the flirtatious handshake. We've discussed how to speak with the right body language, properly work a room, and mirror in subtle ways.

Now it's time to stop the action and *listen*. Why, you ask? Because active listeners make phenomenal flirts (quite the contrary to *untrained* flirts, who think that the more you talk, the better the flirt you are). To gain perspective about the importance of listening, think about how you feel when someone *isn't* listening. The person looks bored, has wandering eyes, and makes comments unrelated to what you just said. As a result, that person doesn't make you feel good.

Now think about how you feel when someone listens intently to you. With eyes and ears tuned to you—and only you—you feel like a super star, like the center of the universe. That's a feeling worth reciprocating, right?

Listening is one of the most valuable parts of the flirting communication process because it creates an interpersonal bond. When you feel that someone has heard you and that s/he truly understands your words and your feelings, you connect with that person, and you want to continue the conversation.

THE ESSENTIALS OF LISTENING

What is there to learn about listening? All you have to do is sit and do nothing, right? No, it's much more than that! Listening is not a passive process. It is as active and alive as talking, and certain rules accompany it.

It's no biological accident that we have two ears and one mouth. It means you should listen twice as much as you talk. This may seem hard for some of you, but it is essential.

Before you can uphold this rule successfully, however, make sure that no barriers—no listening pitfalls—stand in your way. Once you are familiar with these common obstacles, you can easily overcome them and move one step closer to listening enlightenment.

Five main types of barriers get in between people and their ability to listen intently. Let's review each and discuss the best remedies. Once we get these barriers out of the way, we can move straight into my foolproof listening strategy—guaranteed to make you a great flirt.

Listening Barrier #1: Emotions

It can be exciting and scary when someone you've had your eye on approaches you. Your mind races, your heart beats quickly, and anxiety makes listening difficult. Likewise, if something unrelated to your flirting encounter has you preoccupied or worried, you diminish your ability to listen with clarity.

So how do you prevent your emotions from getting the better of you? First, accept that this happens and that it happens to everyone. Nerves get in the way of listening. Push the jitters aside and tell yourself that listening will make flirting easier and more successful. Take a few deep breaths and erase your mind's competing emotions. In this case, a one-track mind *is* your goal.

If you really can't get over your nerves, be open about it and tell your flirting interest that you feel a bit nervous. It will show your human side, and you never know; s/he might tell you the same (in which case suggest taking a walk together if the situation lends itself to this—it's a great calming technique).

Listening Barrier #2: Outside Distractions

Because so much is going on around you when you flirt, it can be hard to zero in on your flirting interest. Some of the most common distractions include other conversations, loud music, other people, or even the room's light and temperature. Tuning out the distractions is challenging but necessary.

Like with your emotions, accept that anywhere you go will have distractions. The key is how you manage them. Try to anticipate distractions—and possible solutions—in advance. This way, you're as prepared as possible to diffuse any that come your way. For example, if you know you're going to a bar or party with loud music, try finding a place to talk far away from the speakers or sound system. If you know you're always cold, bring a jacket or a scarf. If you're always hot, wear layers so you can stay comfortable.

If a distraction arises for which you weren't prepared, remain calm and think on your toes. For example, if someone else's conversation competes with yours, ask your flirting interest if s/he would mind moving somewhere else in the room (an acceptance here means the relationship is going in the right direction). If you think you'd prefer speaking to that nearby guy or gal, be honest and let that person know you see someone else to whom you need to speak. There is no point in half-listening. In fact, it's rude and you are wasting everyone's time. Be fair and move on.

Listening Barrier #3: Mind Wandering

Our minds wander for a myriad of reasons. Maybe you can't stop thinking about your bad day at work, your to-do list, the homework your child still needs to do, or even dinner. No matter the issue, when your mind wanders, you are not in the present and you can't listen attentively—a serious roadblock for flirting banter. Your small talk loses its spontaneity. When your mind takes a temporary vacation, flirting is impossible.

As soon as your mind starts wandering, take a deep breath to regroup, focus your eyes back on your flirting interest, and say, "I'm sorry. I missed what you just said." This will get you back on track and let the other person know that listening is your number one priority. If you think the reason for your wandering mind may make a good conversation topic, use it. For instance, tell your flirting interest about how your bad day at work has left you unable to clear your mind and ask how s/he unwinds and refocuses. This brings the other person back into the conversation and shows that you're interested in his/her opinion and advice.

Listening Barrier #4: Comprehension Difficulties (a.k.a. Pretending to Understand When You Don't)

We are often afraid to admit when we don't understand or know what someone is talking about, such as a sports or political figure, an unusual cocktail, something trendy, a word or expression, or a piece of history. We often nod in agreement, afraid of appearing stupid or out of touch.

But is this the best course of action? Will that make a better impression, or will others like you more if you pretend to hear or understand something your flirting interest has said?

Honesty is one of flirting's golden rules, so you must know that this is absolutely the wrong strategy to take. After all, what if someone calls you on it and turns your "harmless" nod into an awkward moment? Use your lack of knowledge (or "failure to hear") as a flirting opportunity. Admit to the other person that you did not catch or understand what or who s/he was talking about and ask for an explanation or to hear it again. This gives the other person the chance to talk more about the topic and gives you a second chance to listen intently. It also shows that you care about what s/he has to say—and who doesn't love feeling like that?

Listening Barrier #5: The *Next* Rather Than *Now* Focus

Focusing on what to say next rather than listening now turns super flirts into flirts who fall flat. Do not waste your flirting moments figuring out what to say next—it never works. Consider this scenario:

He says: "What's your favorite TV show?"

She says: "Oh, I love Phantom of the Opera."

He says: "Isn't that a Broadway show, not a TV show?"

The issue here is that she only heard part of what he said because she got ahead of herself trying to plan a response. She never heard the word TV and therefore came across as if not paying attention to him.

So how do you stay in the "hear" and now? By focusing on the moment and listening to the words and feelings of your flirting interest. You can also try to maintain better eye contact, or move just a bit closer to your flirting interest—kind of like your teacher used to do when she moved you up to the front of the classroom! By doing this, it will be easier for you to pay close attention. Finally, no matter how great the temptation to plan your retort, don't do it. It's so much easier to be spontaneous, playful, and interesting when you simply *respond appropriately* to what was said.

BE A DYNAMIC AND ACTIVE LISTENER IN THREE STEPS

Now that you know how to deal with barriers, let's get to the task of listening itself. What is listening? Listening can be described as giving your thoughtful attention to another person and being lively, active, and animated in response. It doesn't mean "staring" at another person while s/he talks or being lethargic, apathetic, or listless. Listening is an *action*, and it needs to be right.

Step #1: Give Your Undivided Attention

Remember, it is better to be *interested* than *interesting*! Give your flirting partner your undivided attention by maintaining eye contact and proper distance and above all else listening closely to what s/he says. Tune in your flirting interest and the topic at hand and tune out everything else.

Here are my top tips for giving your undivided attention:

- Laugh at funny comments.
- Nod or say "yes," "right," or "exactly" when you agree with something.
- Listen to the other person's stories, even if you think they are too long, and try your best not to interrupt.
- Move in closer to tell the person you don't want to miss a word.
- Maintain eye contact to show that you are following the conversation.
- Smile to let your flirting interest know that you are enjoying your time together.
- Block out distractions around you.
- Avoid quick glances at your watch.

Step #2: Offer Instantaneous Feedback

This one is really important. Your flirting interest cannot read your mind, but s/he can read your signals. This means you should provide on-the-spot, immediate feedback. Don't make the other person speculate; it ruins the flirting flow.

Keep your listening feedback sweet and simple by using one or more words from the following list: "Yes," "Yeah," "Uh-huh," "I see," "Oh," "Really," and "Wow!" These communicate that you are listening, and encourage your flirting interest to continue. Just remember that timing with these words is important as well. Saying "yes" or "uh-huh" every once in awhile works well; saying it every two seconds can irritate and grate on someone's nerves. Practice moderation.

Step #3: Paraphrase What Your Flirting Interest Said

During a lull or natural pause in the conversation, repeat back what your flirting interest said to keep the conversation engaging and remind your interest that you're all ears.

Restate what s/he said *in your own words*. Don't parrot, but interpret. Make sure that you also paraphrase the feelings as well, if appropriate. This is a great way to maintain a meaningful conversation.

For example, if your flirting interest says, "The traffic was horrendous tonight. It took me two hours to get here when it should have taken me less than an hour. And I got soaked on the way in." You might say, "Wow! It took you two hours?! That sounds awful. You must be beat. And then getting drenched on top of it all? Sounds like that was the icing on the cake."

When you restate, paraphrase, summarize, or interpret what your flirting interest said, you pay him/her the greatest compliment: showing genuine interest and concern. Flirting doesn't get any better than that.

FLIRTING TIP: DEMONSTRATE ADMIRATION

Expressing admiration is also a real turn-on because it showcases your superior listening skills. You can't admire someone if you don't listen to what s/he has to say.

MOVE FOUR

USE FLIRTING PROPS TO GET NOTICED AND START CONVERSATIONS

For your last and final move, let's take some of the pressure off of you and show you how to sit back, relax, and let your props work for you. Consider it my gift to you!

A prop is an accessory that makes a personal statement. It gets others' attention and invites flirting prospects to talk to you. That's why you should never leave home without one. These props are the most natural conversation pieces you'll ever find.

Props work so well because they give others the chance to talk to you about something *tangible*, rather than simply pulling a topic out of thin air. That's right, props make it easier for *other people* to make the first move *on you*; all you have to do is respond and flirt back with interest and energy. I told you it was easy!

THE TOP TEN FLIRTING PROPS ON THE PLANET

Although I love talking to strangers, I love it even more when someone approaches me first. It's great for my ego, very flattering, and nice to just get noticed. Props tremendously increase your chances of getting noticed. They turn you into an instant people-magnet.

My top-ten, cream-of-the-crop props are as follows:

1. Jewelry with a twist
2. Personalized clothing
3. Your scent
4. Manicured nails
5. Shopping bags, totes, and umbrellas
6. Reading material
7. Friendly dogs
8. Kids
9. Cameras
10. Your ring tone

A PROP IS A FLIRTING *MAGNET*

Props attract others to you because they separate you from the crowd and give people a reason to contact you. They're instant attention-grabbers.

FROM THE FLIRTING FIELD

A former student, Jaime, thirty-nine, had a pocketbook with a huge clock on it that actually worked. Wherever she went, both men and women were drawn to it—and *her*—because of its uniqueness. The pocketbook clock helped Jaime have many interesting conversations, several dates, and even some romantic connections.

Prop #1: Jewelry with a Twist

Unique, unusual, different, or even classic jewelry will encourage others to comment. If it makes you stand out, it is the perfect prop. Likewise, if you have a favorite jewelry piece or one you have received compliments on in the past, incorporate it into your prop pile.

Your jewelry "prop" could be old, new, trendy, timeless, homemade, crafty, expensive, a super bargain, or very delicate. It could be a bracelet made out of paper clips from your six-year-old daughter, an antique necklace or a neon pink one, an old watch passed down from your great-grandfather, or a sparkling ring you designed yourself. Basically, any jewelry that complements or enhances your outfit can be a conversation piece.

In my opinion, a watch is the greatest jewelry prop of all—for men and women alike. A watch is the most noticed piece of jewelry because asking the time is a natural way to start a conversation. Once you ask for the time, compliment the watch and continue from there.

Here are a few other examples of jewelry that will stimulate curiosity and small talk. Adapt any of these suggestions to fit your own personal jewelry style. Just remember—dare to be different. It will get you noticed.

- Large gold hoop earrings with a star charm on one earring (flirters will notice the single charm)
- A ring with a dangling charm of your initial, with the letter as an icebreaker
- A pin that showcases your profession or passion (e.g., silver scissors for a hairstylist)
- A necklace with a charm that showcases something you love (e.g., a pair of flip flops to symbolize that you love the summer or the beach)
- Multiple toe rings
- A big and bold watch
- Antique cuff links
- A bracelet made out of candy wrappers, especially if you love candy
- A diving watch
- A trendy piece of jewelry that other trendsetters will notice

Prop #2: Personalized Clothing

Have you ever started a conversation with someone wearing a t-shirt or hat spelling out a place you've visited or a school you attended? That's because the clothing instantaneously gives you common ground, no opening line needed.

Wearing clothing that signifies something about you (e.g., a shirt, baseball cap, jacket, or shorts with your alma mater or your town name) gives your flirting prospect a green light to start talking to you. If your flirting wardrobe lacks these "personalized" items, add at least two or three pieces. (Remember, however, that first and foremost your clothing needs to fit the situation—wearing a college sweatshirt to a black-tie affair is never a good idea.)

FROM THE FLIRTING FIELD

The best flirting clothing includes items with any of the following:

- A place or sightseeing attraction (e.g., the Eiffel Tower or Niagara Falls) that you have visited
- A museum you have explored
- An organization to which you belong (e.g., a volunteer firefighter association or an alumni group)
- An activity club in which you participate (e.g., a triathlon or photography club)
- A political candidate or association you support
- A cause meaningful to you (e.g., saving the environment or fighting breast cancer)
- A hobby or passion (e.g., fishing, dancing, or kite-flying)
- A school you attend or attended

This clothing gives others a little insight into you and your interests. People who share these interests or affiliations will naturally feel more comfortable around you because you already have a bond. And don't forget to wear these items when traveling or on vacation—it's even more fun to get noticed when you are away from home.

Prop #3: Your Scent

The cologne or perfume you wear will draw attention to you. Your scent is your signature because it's based on personal preference. If no one compliments your scent, consider trying another one. But please, don't bathe in it to see whether you get a different reaction.

MAN PROPS: TIES AND SUSPENDERS

When it comes to flirting props, attention-grabbing ties are a man's best friend. Look for well-made silk ties that go well with a suit. Splurge on a few and forego those that pill easily or don't tie well. And don't be afraid to wear colorful or unusual ties—you want them to get noticed. The same goes for suspenders (if that's more your style)—the funkier, the better! Make them your conversation piece.

Prop #4: Manicured Nails

Whether you are a gal or guy, people notice your hands all the time—that's why having well manicured nails will take you far. It's a sign that you value your appearance and take pride in yourself.

Manicure doesn't always equal painted nails. For guys, this means keeping your nails clean and trimmed. For ladies, the same thing goes, but you may also consider a French manicure, sheer polish, seasonal color, nail jewelry, or a subtle design. A professional manicure may be one of your best flirting investments.

Prop #5: Shopping Bags, Totes, and Umbrellas

You probably need to carry a few of these items anyway, so why not make them unique? Try a shopping bag from a specialty shop, a tote from a conference you attended, or a colorful umbrella (i.e., one that is not black).

Someone is much more likely to strike up a conversation if your tote conveys the name of something they relate to or can identify with.

Prop #6: Reading Material

Ever been on a subway or train reading and had someone comment on your literary selection? It happens all the time, right? That's why reading material makes the perfect prop—it shows others *two* of your interests: reading and the subject about which you're reading. Plus, it invites recommendations.

Choose a book, magazine, or newspaper that interests you. It could be your text book, this book, a rare magazine, a journal to which you subscribe, a foreign language newspaper, essays by your favorite author, or a current bestseller—the more out of the ordinary, controversial, or trendy, the better. You never know; the next time you carry your favorite book may be the best time of your life.

THE GIFT WRAP MATTERS

How you put yourself together speaks volumes about you. What do you want to portray? A well-wrapped package entices the recipient to open it. If you want flirting prospects to flock to you, take the time to package yourself well.

Prop #7: Friendly Dogs

If you have a pet—or don't mind walking your friend's—this one is a winner. What it is about dogs that compels us to say hello to them? Who knows, but let's go with it!

A pooch is a great flirting accessory because people who stop to admire or pet your dog already show you that you have something in common—your love for canines. As s/he talks to Fido, chime in with questions about whether s/he also owns a pet or his/her favorite breed.

If you don't have or want a pet, offer your dog-sitting or dog-walking services to your friends. You'll not only be helpful, but you may even get a date out of it.

Prop #8: Kids

Children under the age of five are natural flirts—everyone wants to get a smile out of them! With kids around, there is so much to talk about, especially if the other person has a child as well. After chatting about your kids, it's easy to move the conversation to you, your relationship status, your interests, and so on.

If you don't have small children and you are a capable, responsible babysitter, consider taking a niece or nephew, godchild, or friend's child out for an afternoon at the mall, park, or playground. You'll have fun no matter what.

Prop #9: Cameras

Carrying a camera, especially and social events and attractions where snapping shots is acceptable, certainly puts the attention on you. People will wonder whether you are a tourist, a photographer, a reporter covering a news story, or whether you know about something going on that they don't and should.

Get the conversation started by asking someone to take your photo (especially if you really are a tourist) or by apologizing for the bright flash and explaining why you're taking the shots.

Prop #10: Your Ring Tone

Pick an unforgettable ring tone, such as your favorite song or a funny sound (like an old-fashioned phone ringing, a bird chirping, or a person whistling). It will grab people's attention and cause them to ask you about it.

Make sure the sound is not too loud or jarring and that it goes off *before* the two of you start chatting—you don't want your sassy ring to interrupt the conversation flow; you want it to be the *reason for* a great conversation. Use this prop in a venue like a bar or other loud place where a phone sounding isn't considered rude.

PROPS GO BOTH WAYS

As you've learned, props are tools of your trade. They increase your flirting possibilities and look great on too.

Props can go both ways. Instead of waiting for others to comment about *your* props, comment about *theirs*! It's an easy, fun way to kick-start a conversation. And who doesn't love talking about him/herself?

EASY PROP-RELATED QUESTIONS YOU CAN DELIVER

Think of another person's prop as your cue card—it tells you what to say. Although you don't have a script, consider props as clues to solving a puzzle. The more questions you ask, the more information you get, and the better the flirting becomes. And as you learn more about the other person, you will find more topics in common and the conversation will soar. It's simple as pie.

Here are some examples of great ways to use props as conversation starters:

- "Your necklace is beautiful. Is that vintage?"
- "I just wanted to tell you your cuff links looks so posh. You hardly ever see guys sporting them anymore, which is a shame."
- "Did you go to UCLA? I have almost the exact same t-shirt."
- "Are you wearing Armani? You smell so nice."
- "I just love the design you have on your nails. How did they create that?"
- "Where did you find that great tote? Is it really made from 100 percent recycled material?"
- "How do find that book so far? I had a hard time getting into it at first but ended up loving it."
- "Do you subscribe to that magazine? They ran a really touching article about [insert topic] a few months back. Maybe you read it?"
- "Your dog is beautiful. What breed is she?"
- "Your camera looks like it has all the bells and whistles. I'm in the market for one myself; are you happy with that brand?"
- "Ha! Is your ring tone really Bruce Springsteen? That is such a great tune."

CHAPTER TWO

FLIRTING HICCUPS—YOU CAN GET OVER THEM!

NOW THAT YOU'VE LEARNED ALL THE MOVES, TRICKS, AND TECHNIQUES to being a flirting expert, it's time to tackle the more difficult aspects of flirting: the blunders and dealing with the dreaded *R* word, rejection. Learning how to handle these is vital to your flirting health. And though we can't completely prevent them from happening, we can certainly minimize their negative side effects by being prepared.

In this chapter, you will learn the following lessons:

- Flirting when you don't feel well may make you sicker.
- Flirting after an argument will only cause additional fighting.
- Feeling desperate for a date will make it impossible for you to find one.
- Using the wrong words will turn off your flirting interest.
- Spilling the beans too quickly is risky.
- Spending too much time flirting online can lead to unnecessary disappointment.

That's the bad news. The good news is that I will also offer remedies for all of these. I told you that you were in good hands!

THE TOP-FIVE FLIRTING FAUX PAS

From the beginning of this book, my mantra has been flirt, flirt, flirt. Although I want flirting to become second nature for you, I also must warn you that some situations don't warrant flirting. Learn to avoid these five, however, and you will put yourself on a path to flirting triumph. Remember, prevention is the best medicine.

FLIRTING FAUX PAS #1: FLIRTING AT THE WRONG TIME

Hard as it may be to believe, there are times when flirting is not good for you or anyone around you. Either you aren't in the right mood, the timing is off, or you're flirting for the wrong reasons.

Knowing when *not* to flirt will actually help you become a better flirt. It may sound contradictory, but think about it: Instances during which you shouldn't be flirting but do will be flirting disasters. And we all know that flirting failures aren't good for your flirting ego.

During off-limit times (a.k.a., flirting timeouts), give your flirting a rest and work on getting over whatever obstacle is impeding you. There will be many more great flirting opportunities ahead, so don't worry!

So when should you give flirting a rest?

- When you don't feel well
- After an argument
- When you feel desperate

In all of these instances—which we'll discuss in greater detail in the following pages—you are simply not at your best. And because you don't have the "flirting strength" to flirt naturally and with full attention, it's best to just give it rest.

Wrong Time #1: When You Don't Feel Well

This is a time when you feel needy, cranky, demanding, and clingy, and you're the only person on your mind. Because flirting is not about you but rather about the person with whom you are flirting, it's easy to see the problem.

When you have the flu, a splitting headache, or are jet lagged, emotionally exhausted, or feeling out of sorts, it will be impossible to act playful and confident—two essential flirting ingredients. Rather than flirt, heal yourself. It's a win-win situation for everyone!

FROM THE FLIRTING FIELD

Debi, thirty-one, just had a huge argument with her ex-husband. Although she was angry and bitter, she decided to go to the bookstore to try to forget about the argument.

At the store, as Debi reached for a book, she dropped her car keys. As she went to retrieve them, a man next to her quickly reached down and picked them up for her. "I could have gotten those," Debi grunted as she walked off.

Then she went to get a cup of coffee. As she ordered, a man next to her asked her whether the coffee there was fresh. Nastily, Debi blurted out, "How would I know? I'm standing in line behind you," and the conversation quickly ended.

Debi sat down to drink her coffee. She saw a man who intrigued her, so she asked him a question about the book he was holding. He gave her a short answer and continued reading. Sarcastically, Debi said to herself, "Is that all you could say?" and left the bookstore worse off than when she arrived.

Debi had no clue that she was her own worst enemy. Because of her negativity and anger, any flirting attempts turned into mini-arguments. Don't let this happen to you.

Wrong Time #2: After an Argument

Anger and flirting do not mix. You may think flirting while angry is no big deal and that you will easily ignore or forget about your emotions, but as soon as you get the slightest twinge of rejection, your hostility could bubble up and cause an explosion. You may unwittingly snap at an unsuspecting flirting prospect.

Being angry and bitter makes a scapegoat out of whoever comes your way. When your mood is heavy, serious, and depressed, stay away from flirting and get back to it when your feelings subside.

Wrong Time #3: When You Feel Desperate

Have you ever found yourself compelled to flirt because you desperately needed a date for something? This is not the time to flirt. *Desperate* screams needy, turns people off, and scares away any possibilities.

When you feel pressure to meet someone—you need a date for your boss' holiday party or you found out that your boyfriend of two months cheated on you—but your only flirting motive is to get revenge or to find anyone to take to the party, take a step back and regroup.

FLIRTING TIP: FLIRT WITHOUT A CAUSE

Your chances of getting a date rise exponentially when you aren't desperate to get one. You might think that if you are desperate, you will work harder to find a date, but what will come across first and foremost is your hopeless, frantic vibe, which is a total turn-off.

Focus on the fun of flirting instead of getting a date or a phone number, and you might just find that "luck" ends up on your side.

FLIRTING FAUX PAS #2: FLIRTING WITH THE WRONG WORDS

Have you ever regretted saying something the second it came out of your mouth? Something so off the mark that the look on other person's face told you it definitely wasn't cool? We all have, and when this occurs, it's best to have a strategy on hand for a quick recovery (or better yet, read this section ahead of time to keep them from happening at all).

Following are a few verbal blunders to avoid at all costs as well as a few strategies to use in case of a slip-up. Remember, anything is fixable.

Using Unfriendly or Negative Opening Lines

Stay away from opening lines with a negative spin. They make your flirting prospect defensive, and no matter how innocent your intentions, you will get shot down. Here are some examples of what *not* to say:

- "What's a nice gal/guy like you doing in a place like this?" (conversation killer)
- "Didn't you have anything better to do tonight than come here?" (insulting and a put-down)
- "Haven't I seen you at singles workshops before? Still haven't met anyone? (a personal dig—and hypocritical!)
- "What a boring bunch of people here!" (back-handed and in poor taste)
- "Why are you so dressed up?" (confusing and uncomfortable)

In the rare instance you find yourself accidentally uttering something you wish you hadn't said, here's how you can quickly turn that blooper into a gem.

First, apologize. Say that you did not mean to offend, and rephrase your question into a compliment. For example, after saying, "How come you are so dressed up?" make amends by saying, "I'm sorry, what I really wanted to say was that your dress is outrageously cool." Or after saying, "Haven't I seen you at singles workshops before? Still haven't met anyone?" quickly recover with, "Sorry, disregard that. What I meant was that I'm glad you're here tonight because I wanted to introduce myself to you a few weeks ago but didn't get the chance."

Giving the Gory Details

Have you ever found yourself telling your life story to your flirting interest before you even know his/her name? Trust me, it's never a good idea. TMI (too much information) only leads to infinite awkward moments, and by the end, you both feel uneasy (and you can't take back what you said).

FROM THE FLIRTING FIELD

Josh, a thirty-three-year-old pharmacist, didn't have a date to his cousin's wedding. Josh never enjoyed going to weddings alone and was fraught with anxiety at the thought of not having a date. Luckily, he was attending a singles expo at a local hotel a few days before the wedding. Josh was ecstatic at the prospect of meeting someone there he could take.

Josh eagerly began making conversations with the women at the expo. Within three minutes of talking to someone, he would ask her to the wedding. Each woman said no. When Josh and I discussed this during a coaching session later, he said, "I thought if I asked enough women, *someone* would have agreed to go."

I asked Josh to tell me the names of the five women to whom he spoke and one fact about each one. He couldn't do either. What he did recall, though, was one saying, "You don't even know me, why would you want to go to a wedding with me?"

Josh and I discussed the implications of that statement. He now understood that he appeared needy and desperate. We talked about how weddings are often the perfect place to flirt and how next time Josh gets invited to one, instead of frantically trying to get a date, he'll have a great time going solo.

Still on the fence? Allow me to give you an example. Roseann, thirty-nine, meets Simon, forty-three, at a wedding rehearsal dinner. The two start chatting and Roseann asks Simon whether he has ever been married. Simon says yes, but that he's been divorced for five years—and that the bitterness and hurt has never gone away.

Simon: "I was madly in love with my wife and she told me that she didn't love me anymore and that it was time to go our separate ways. In two weeks, she was gone, the bank accounts were emptied, and she came into the house when I was away on business and took anything and everything she could get her hands on. I'm not sure if I can ever trust women again. Even dating is painful for me."

Roseann: "Oh, wow, what a story. Sorry, but I see my cousin over there—I should go say hi. Take care."

What advice would you give Simon?

My advice would be this: Save the heavy emotions for another day much further down the line and first make a connection with Roseann. Start getting to know each other *slowly*. I'm not suggesting that you be dishonest, but take your time with all the burdensome details. (As for Roseann, she acted as best she could in this situation and removed herself from the conversation quickly and without drama.

If Simon could have a do-over, his conversation may go something like this:

Roseann: "Have you ever been married?"

Simon: "Yes. I've been divorced for about five years."

Roseanne: "Oh really?"

Simon: "Yeah, we grew apart and were no longer happy, so we moved on. I'm enjoying getting out there now and meeting new people. What about you? Has marriage been in your past—or do you perhaps see it in your future?"

Going Overboard While Flirting Online

Flirting online—via email, an online dating site, and so on—is a great way to break the ice with a potential interest, but it also can be tricky territory. Without face-to-face contact, people sometimes feel they can say anything because they are talking to a "blank screen." If you wouldn't say something in person, don't type it.

Also, make sure that to be honest when flirting online. Be yourself and resist the temptation to exaggerate details—about your work, personality, age, weight, or looks. Being untruthful will only create unrealistic expectations and could even lead to an uncomfortable first face-to-face meeting.

Use your online interactions to ignite sparks, but try not to rely on emails for too long. As soon as you are both comfortable and eager, make the move to talking on the phone, or arrange a time and place to meet in person. The longer you put it off, the greater the risk of skewed expectations.

FLIRTING TIP: PUT YOURSELF IN HIS/HER SHOES

Think for a moment about how you would feel if someone buttered you up and then hightailed it out of there. Chances are, you'd feel really bummed out and maybe even angry at yourself for being so nice.

Don't let this happen to you, and, even more importantly, don't be the cause of these feelings for others. Always remember that flirting must be honest, and never about what you will gain at your flirting interest's expense.

FLIRTING FAUX PAS #3: FLIRTING TO MANIPULATE SOMEONE

As I've said before, flirting should be sincere, genuine, and honest. It should not be a way to trick someone into doing something for you. If I started to flirt with you at a bar just to get a drink out of you and ditched you once I got the drink or if I flirted with you in a ticket line so I could get a closer spot and then ignored you, I wasn't truly flirting, but rather scheming and calculating.

Avoid this trap by asking yourself one simple question before you make your first move: Why do I want to flirt with this person? If you determine it's because you're genuinely interested, flirt on. If, however, it's just to snag the open seat next to him/her, get something for free, or get inside quicker because s/he knows the guy at the door, let it go! You'll both be glad you did.

FLIRTING FAUX PAS #4: FLIRTING WITH WANDERING EYES

We have all experienced this: You start talking to who appears to be a really nice man or woman, but soon into the conversation, his/her eyes are everywhere except focused on you. It's not a good feeling. (I wouldn't dare dream that *you* would do something like this, especially now that you're a flirting aficionado!)

If this happens to you, however, ignore it for a few minutes at most. If it continues, confront it head on with a question such as "Is there something distracting you?" If the wandering eyes continue, confidently say that you need to get going. Or if you're feeling bold, say something such as, "It seems that you are more interested in what's going on around you than us talking, so I'm going to go mingle."

Because at times we all get distracted, if you feel it might be worth it, give him/her a second chance. If it happens again, however, say adios for good!

"THE GREATER THE SPONTANEITY, THE BETTER THE FLIRTING WILL BE."

FLIRTING FAUX PAS #5: FLIRTING WITH THE FUTURE IN MIND

In all likelihood, your flirting will eventually generate real sparks with someone. In these instances, keep the fire going but don't let your imagination get ahead of you. Don't think about where the two of you could go on your honeymoon or what you'll name your kids. This will ruin the moment without a doubt. The more you project into the future—even if only in your mind—the less likely you will focus on enjoying the flirting banter. Let flirting take its natural course. If the wedding registry is meant to be, you'll be the first to know.

MAKE REJECTION WORK FOR YOU

This sounds impossible and unrealistic, right? I promise you—it's not!

I despise rejection. I have never been good at accepting it. But rejection is universal—no one escapes it, no matter how much you think it only happens to you.

The worst part of rejection is that it makes you doubt yourself; all of your insecurities rise to the surface. No matter how much you try to push them away, you still feel lousy and dejected. You say to yourself: "Why me?" "What did I do to make this happen?" "If only I acted differently," "What if I tried harder?" and so on.

Sure, rejection can be immobilizing and painful. But the minute you let it control you, it will hold you back from getting the love you want. Don't give it that power.

REAL VS. REEL REJECTION

Have you been rejected by a boyfriend, girlfriend, spouse, or friend? Most of us have, and we know getting over that hurt can be slow, agonizing, and time-consuming. Relationship rejection takes its toll, but when you do overcome it, you get your life back.

Flirting rejection can sometimes feel as devastating as real rejection. How can this be? How could you feel truly rejected by a stranger? Easily. Allow me to explain.

When rejected during flirting, your life's "movie reel" starts playing. All of your previous "real rejections" bubble up and replay in your mind. You remember how awful it felt. Somehow this little flirting rejection gets blown out of proportion and starts feeling like your previous real rejections.

Rejection's sorrow and hurt are awful and devastating. To deal with rejection, have a coping plan in place—I call it the "reframing rejection" plan. It's worked wonders for me, and I'm sure it will do the same for you.

ALL FLIRTS EXPERIENCE REJECTION: IT'S NOT JUST YOU

When people around you experience flirting rejection, do you notice or care? I know you probably think that everyone around you knows when you have been rejected, but honestly, the only person who knows, cares, or is the least bit interested is you.

Others couldn't care less. "They" don't know it happened, don't care if it happened, and because they are so focused on everything else are not paying attention to your rejection. They are obsessing about their own flirting moves, so stop worrying about them and move on.

THE REFRAMING REJECTION PLAN

Fear of rejection stops us from flirting, and we can't let that happen. Instead, turn rejection from your enemy into your friend. My Reframing Rejection Plan will do just that. All it takes is an open mind.

Step #1: Redefine

The fact is that one out of every three people with whom you flirt will not be interested in you. We can't change these odds. What we can change is your perspective.

To put flirting rejection into perspective, redefine it. Flirting rejection is nothing more than a person not being interested in you. It doesn't mean you are a bad person or that something is wrong with you. For whatever reason, you are not your rejecter's cup of tea. It's his/her loss for not being interested, not yours.

Although the rejection stings, lucky you to cross him/her off your potential-mates list. Since when should everybody be interested in everybody else? Are you?

The person who rejects you actually does you a favor by ditching you. S/he helps you in your quest to find the right person. It's better to know now than in two months or two years that someone isn't really interested. (And the funny part is, when you do meet your soul mate, you won't care at all about past rejections. In fact, you'll be glad you got them!)

Instead of seeing someone "passing you up" as a rejection, see it as a gift that has given you an instant "weed-out" of someone not right for you, the time to make more connections, and an opportunity to meet people truly interested in you.

Step #2: Respond

Let's say someone with whom you were hoping to establish a connection rejects you. What do you do now? Should you be nasty, feel sorry for yourself, or dwell on why s/he didn't like you?

The answer is none of the above. Maintain your dignity, self-respect, and self-confidence. After your "interest-no-more" gives you the rejection red light (e.g., gives one-word answers to your questions, sighs every so often, fidgets, looks at his/her watch, etc.), politely say that you have to get going and move on.

Keep your expectations in the here and now, and it won't even feel like rejection.

Step #3: Walk Away and Forget About It Forever

As you walk away, tell yourself that your rejecter did you a favor and thank him/her—in your head, not aloud—for not wasting your time. Don't dwell on the rejection. It gets you nowhere and this person does not deserve any more of your time or energy. Instead, turn your rejection into motivation to keep looking.

Continue mingling and having fun. If you see someone else who looks interesting, approach him/her. Remember, the best "revenge" is your happiness. Although rejection hurts, only 10 percent of the problem comes from the rejection itself. The other 90 percent is your attitude.

FLIRTING TIP: WHEN IT COMES TO REJECTION, ORDER YOURS SMALL

Rejection comes in all sizes: small, medium, large, and extra large. It is not one-size-fits-all. What is your rejection size? The more you blame yourself for your flirting interest not wanting you, the larger you grow your rejection size, and the more debilitating it becomes. Make your rejection an extra-small by not letting it get to you at all.

DEALING WITH ONLINE FLIRTING REJECTION

My clients who use online dating sites, both men and women, complain about online flirting rejection all the time. They say they are being proactive, sending engaging emails, and so on, yet nothing happens. They get no response, not even a "no thanks." They get frustrated and discouraged, and they often tell me that online dating is too much work without enough reward.

But this happens; it's part of the online dating experience—you may have even done this to someone yourself. For a gazillion reasons, sometimes you just won't get a response. Although it feels disappointing, discouraging, and frustrating, you have to expect it.

Rather than ruminating over those who don't respond, invest your efforts into making new connections and replying to responses you do get. There are plenty of fish in the electronic sea—the trick is to keep casting your line.

A FINAL NOTE ABOUT CELEBRATING REJECTION

Being rejected ultimately helps you get closer to finding the love that you want and deserve. You unequivocally don't want to be with someone who doesn't want you. You want to be with someone who shows interest and excitement at the prospect of getting to know you from the flirting start.

Don't give rejection more power than it deserves. Don't let it stop you from searching for love. Instead, let it drive you to find the one who realizes just how worth it you are!

FLIRTING TIP: FOLLOW-UP IF YOU MUST, THEN LET IT GO

If there is someone online who you really want to communicate with *(meet)*, you may send a second email if s/he doesn't respond to your first one. But if you still don't receive a response after that, let it go. It wasn't meant to be.

CHAPTER THREE

WHERE TO FLIRT—THE THIRTY-FIVE BEST FLIRTING SPOTS

THE BEST PLACE TO FLIRT IS ANYWHERE AND EVERYWHERE! But you want specifics, right? Well that's why I'm here!

This chapter will take you through my top thirty-five flirting spots, which are based on all of the great stories I have been told by thousands of flirting workshop participants, as well as my very own flirting expeditions. Not a day goes by that I haven't flirted several times and in several locations, and I encourage you to take my advice and do the same! You have every-thing to gain.

THE TOP THIRTY-FIVE PLACES TO FLIRT

Using all you've learned, you should be able to vary your flirting spots with ease and try different strategies in different situations.

Note that these thirty-five places are in no particular ranked order because "top" spots vary immensely from person to person and are largely influenced by your lifestyle, habits, and where you live. A place of worship or a commuter train, for example, may not make your "top ten," but it might for someone else, so just remember to zero in on those places that fit best with your lifestyle.

LOCATION #1: THE BOOKSTORE

The bookstore combines the best of the flirting elements: endless props to discuss, many people by themselves, often a café to grab a cup of coffee, and places to sit.

The next time you're at a bookstore, walk around. When you spot a flirting prospect, start looking at similar books and let your inquiring mind take over. Ask for help selecting a book or offer your opinion about a topic or author.

LOCATION #2: THE MALL OR CLOTHING SHOP

Ask directions for a store that you "can't find" (I won't tell). Ladies, go to the men's department of a store and seek advice on "a tie for your cousin." Men, go to the ladies department and ask for help selecting a "gift for your aunt's birthday." Grab a bite at the food court and start chatting about the crowds and the food.

LOCATION #3: THE PARK

The park is full of people out having a good time and getting some fresh air—and you can't ask for a more positive vibe than that! If you see someone who looks friendly and approachable, don't be afraid to start a conversation. You never know where it could lead!

LOCATION #4: BARS, PUBS, AND CLUBS

From after-work happy hours to thirty-something Thursdays to ladies' night Wednesdays, there is always something going on at a bar, pub, or club, which makes these places great for practicing your skills. Find a spot at the bar, order a drink, and talk to people around you. Work the bar by strolling around as if going somewhere and stopping when you have reached your "destination."

LOCATION #5: THE BEACH

Where there is water, there is flirting. Head for the beach, lake, or town pool with a few friends to scope out the possibilities. Wear sunscreen with a delicious smell, and don't forget your props (e.g., magazines or a book, water toys, or even a beach towel from your university or a previous travel destination). Spend some time at the concession stand too—it's always a great place to meet someone.

LOCATION #6: WHEREVER YOU EXERCISE

The gym or park you work out in is the perfect location to flex your flirting muscles. Why you ask? Because even if you see someone to whom you want to talk but don't get the opportunity, chances are you will see him/her again.

When you do, say, "Hi, I noticed you last week but didn't have an opportunity to introduce myself. I'm Tracy," or something to that effect. Ask for help with a particular machine, talk about your workout routine, or compliment the other person on his/her fitness ability or dedication. We all know a compliment can take you far!

LOCATION #7: PARTIES

The great thing about a party is the collective upbeat mood. The best party has many people you don't know—because that equals many more flirting moments. Don't be shy, act as outgoing as the host, and make others feel welcome. Your good vibes will draw others to you.

FLIRTING TIP: EARN SOME MILEAGE

As a frequent flirter, you are sure to rack up hundreds of flirting miles. And how lucky you are! Because the more you "travel" (flirt), the closer you'll be to finding the love of your life.

LOCATION #8: THE SUPERMARKET, LOCAL MARKET, OR SPECIALTY SHOP

Food—we all need it and we all love it. What I love most about the supermarket is the many flirting opportunities. In the salad dressing aisle, ask for a suggestion; in the produce section, discuss how to pick a ripe fruit. If you're a tall individual, help someone get an item down from the top shelf. Follow the shopping carts full of prepared foods, single-serving items, or ice cream pints—those are good indicators that your interest sometimes eats solo.

LOCATION #9: ONLINE

Your online words equal flirtatious body language, a warm smile, an inviting personality, and a gentle touch. But because you don't have the visual clues, it will take some creativity and spontaneity to make your flirting come alive on the computer screen. (Some may even like the absence of initial face-to-face contact because it makes flirting easier and because s/he can add and delete until the perfect flirtatious email comes out.)

Your online flirting goal is to make a connection, show interest, and have fun, all with a bit of mystery. Here are few tips:

- Be specific. Comment about something in his/her profile that impressed you, made you smile, is a shared interest, or is something about which you want to know more.

- Use humor. Let your wit show. If s/he says s/he runs four miles a day, say something like, "If I ran one mile, you'd have to carry me for the next three."

- Use compliments. Don't go overboard, but a sincere, unexpected compliment will work wonders.

- Refrain from going on and on. A short email will go a long way. Write enough to show who you are and your desires, and then ask a few questions about him/her. Remember, you aren't writing your autobiography or conducting an interview for a magazine story.

- Spell check, please. A typo here and there is no big deal, but an email riddled with spelling errors and typos is a big turn-off. It says that you did not take the time nor do you have the desire to make a good impression.

- Use punctuation carefully. It can vary the meaning of what you are saying. The following three sentences, for instance, imply three totally different meanings: "Shopping with you sounds fun?" "Shopping with you sounds fun!" and "Shopping with you sounds fun..."

- Close with intrigue. Tell your interest how happy you are to have met him/her and that you look forward to your next chat, phone call, or meeting. Avoid anything that may come across as creepy such as "I'll be waiting here until you come back" or "I won't be able to think of anything else until we talk again." You may mean that in a sweet way, but it sounds off-putting.

LOCATION #10: CLASS

It could be in your freshman English class, your graduate course in architecture, or a wine-tasting, kickboxing, defensive driving, or sightseeing-in-London-on-a-shoe-string-budget class. No matter what, with the playing field leveled, this is a perfect opportunity to flirt! You are all there for the same reason.

Talk with a flirting interest before, during (quietly, of course), or after class. Then suggest going for a drink, coffee, or a bite to eat to discuss what you have just learned!

LOCATION #11: WAITING IN LINE

We spend endless hours waiting in lines—at the bank, motor vehicle office, movies, return counters, post office, amusement parks, and so on. If you are anything like me, you probably want to multitask to make the most of the boring situation. This is where flirting comes in. You have people all around you, you have the time, and you have something in common about which to complain (one of the only times I encourage complaining)! Don't stand in silence. Start flirting—s/he will appreciate your multitasking sort of mind.

LOCATION #12: JURY DUTY

Jury duty can be deadly or divine—it's your choice. Take advantage of the "captive" audience. Find a jury buddy with whom to eat lunch. You never know where it may lead.

LOCATION #13: THE LAUNDROMAT

First do a subtle check to see what's in his/her laundry basket. Depending on what you see, you will know how to proceed. If you determine the laundry contains only his/her clothing, feel free to offer your folding assistance, stain-removal tips, fabric softener, or some flirtatious conversation.

LOCATION #14: THE COFFEE SHOP

When you see someone who looks your type, make eye contact and smile. If you get a return smile, wait for his/her turn to order and say, "It's on me." If s/he resists or says, "How nice of you, are you sure?" you can reply, "If you really want to repay me, how about we have our coffee together?"

LOCATION #15: BUSINESS SEMINARS, TRADE SHOWS, AND CONVENTIONS

These are perfect places to hand out your business cards and make both professional and personal connections. When and if the opportunity arises (and only if appropriate), subtly let some of your business contacts know that you are also in the market for a date (an after-hours cocktail party or get-together would work best).

LOCATION #16: PARENT–TEACHER NIGHT

Talking about your kids with other parents is a great way to break the ice. It is certainly a common denominator—but check for a wedding ring before you make any real moves.

LOCATION #17: THE GAS STATION

Go to a self-service gas station and ask for help pumping your gas, strike up a conversation with the attendant, or ask for directions even if you don't need them.

LOCATION #18: WEDDINGS

Love is in the air at weddings. During the cocktail hour or reception, work the room and introduce yourself to as many people as you can. At your table, make sure you introduce yourself to everyone. If you feel like dancing and don't have a partner, ask someone!

LOCATION #19: THE WAITING ROOM

Instead of reading yesterday's newspaper or an outdated magazine, start talking to someone about the doctor, dentist, or physical therapist who you are waiting to see. Your flirting will take off in no time.

LOCATION #20: THE MUSEUM

Museums offer so much—culture, art, history, and so many potential flirting interests. Pay as much attention to the priceless paintings as you do the priceless company. Ask a flirting interest about the exhibit or remark about the uniqueness of one of the sculptures. While you're complimenting the artifacts, compliment your flirting prospect as well.

LOCATION #21: COMMUTER TRAINS

Feeling a bit shy about talking to the man or woman who always sits in the first seat? Plan it out. Today, smile as you pass by; tomorrow, say hi; and the next day, start a conversation. You have the entire train ride to plan your next flirtatious move.

LOCATION #22: AIRPORTS/PLANES

Turn a boring four-hour airport delay or a short plane ride into a thrilling flirting adventure. Your shared destination already gives you something in common.

LOCATION #23: HOUSES OF WORSHIP

Flirting where you feel comfortable makes flirting fun! Churches and temples also frequently offer great singles events.

LOCATION #24: ELECTRONIC AND HARDWARE STORES
(FOR WOMEN ESPECIALLY)

Men flock to stores like these. If you need the latest electronic gadget or want to meet men, go where they go.

LOCATION #25: A VOLUNTEERING GIG

Shared passion about a cause draws people to each other, and helping others can lead to getting something for yourself as well.

LOCATION #26: SPORTS-RELATED EVENTS

Whether you are watching an event, participating in one, or learning how to play a game, sports-minded people gravitate toward each other. Use it to your advantage.

LOCATION #27: SINGLES EVENTS

Don't wait for someone to flirt with you. Take charge of your social life and make it happen. You have made the effort to attend an event like this, now cash in on the love that could be waiting for you.

LOCATION #28: FAST FOOD PLACES/RESTAURANTS

Fast food places attract people dining alone. If you sit down next to a solo diner and feel like flirting, go for it! At a busy restaurant with a long wait time, forget about your hunger pains by flirting.

LOCATION #29: SUPPORT GROUPS

Although a difficult life event brings you to a support group, flirting can uplift your spirits. Take it slow and concentrate on making the other person feel good—you'll both be glad you did.

LOCATION #30: THE DOG PARK

Dog lovers seek out dog parks where their canine companions can have fun. This puts their owners in a similar frame of mind. Grab your dog (or your best friend's dog) and go for some exercise—just don't forget to exercise your flirting skills as well!

LOCATION #31: YOUR CLASS REUNION

Even if you feel hesitant to attend, go! No one is the same person s/he was five, ten, or twenty years ago, and you never know with whom you might bond or reconnect. Plus, it's always great to find out what happened to your secret crush or old flame, isn't it?

LOCATION #32: A FLEA MARKET, STREET FAIR, OR GARAGE SALE

As you stroll and browse, don't forget to check out your flirting prospects along the way. They could be your most valuable find of the day.

LOCATION #33: SPEED-DATING EVENTS

Because you only have several minutes to spend with your speed-dating partner, make him/ her feel special in your presence. Before the bell rings, make it clear that you would love to get together again (only if you honestly do, of course). With all the tips and tricks you now have up your sleeve, the few minutes you have together should be plenty of time to spark a connection.

LOCATION #34: ON VACATION

Sightseeing may be the highlight of your vacation, but flirting will add to your memories—and may even last a lifetime! According to ShermansTravel.com, the top ten spots for singles include Amsterdam, "at sea" (i.e., a cruise), Buenos Aires, Juneau (Alaska), Las Vegas, Miami, New York, Rome, Tokyo, and Washington, D.C. Plan accordingly!

LOCATION #35: WHEREVER *YOU* ARE

The flirting field is always ready. It is indoors, outdoors, across town, or halfway around the world. Make time every day to get onto the field and play. No matter how far-fetched it sounds, don't wait for the "perfect time" or a special occasion. Flirts on the prowl make flirting a way of life. That means you. No matter where you go, never miss a flirting moment!

CHAPTER FOUR

FLIRTING FINALE—TAKE THE SHOW ON THE ROAD!

ARE YOU READY? YES, OF COURSE YOU ARE! You are ready to face the flirting troops. You are ready to make meeting people a reality. You are ready to win the world over with your charm! But before you go, don't forget to take these Ten Commandments with you.

THE FLIRTING BIBLE'S TEN COMMANDMENTS

1. Make a flirting commitment to yourself.
2. Enjoy your every flirting move.
3. Respect your flirting interest and value yourself.
4. Take an occasional break to rejuvenate.
5. Learn from those with whom you flirt.
6. Accept that sometimes, you will not be interested (and vice versa), but always be kind.
7. Concentrate on one flirting interest at a time.
8. Focus on making your flirting interest feel special.
9. Be honest.
10. Believe that flirting works!

MY FINAL WORDS ABOUT FLIRTING

Flirting is truly an art. It is up to you to give it your own signature. As you flirt, think of me. Know that I am always there in spirit to support and guide you. Flirting is the beginning of your relationship journey—make it start with a bang!

May all your flirtatious encounters be filled with happiness, and may your future be filled with love. Enjoy your journey!

THE ULTIMATE **NONVERBAL** RECIPE FOR FLIRTING SUCCESS

Ingredients:
- 1 smile
- Several glances
- 1 wink
- 1 flirtatious handshake
- Laughter, for sprinkling

Combine together, add a light touch, and top with a lean forward. Mix well and cook for 30 minutes. Continue cooking to suit your taste. Enjoy!

THE ULTIMATE VERBAL RECIPE FOR FLIRTING SUCCESS

Ingredients:

- 1 clever opening line
- 2 to 4 open-ended questions
- 3 to 4 disclosures about yourself

Cook on a warm setting and then turn up heat. Comes out best when topped with plenty of genuine compliments!

ACKNOWLEDGMENTS

There is no better place to start than thanking Will Kiester, my publisher, for having the vision of *The Flirting Bible* and for letting me make my dream of writing a book on flirting a reality. Will, thanks for believing in me and making it happen. Your taste is impeccable!

Mom, you taught me everything about flirting I could ever want to learn. I would not be the flirt I am today were it not for you. Your love, charisma, wisdom, infectious laugh, positive spin on life, and the interest you always had in all of my flirting endeavors are the foundation for this book. If only you could be here to share this milestone with me! I know you are smiling down on me and saying "Franny, I told you so." Thanks Mom, I love you so much for being the best mother any daughter could ever ask for!

To my dad, Joe Greene, who always flirted with my mom and made her feel so special all the time. Dad, thanks for making me feel like a million bucks and for all your love. I know you would be so proud of me!

I saved the best for last: my loving and supportive husband, Jim Mullin, who has been my biggest cheerleader since the day we met. Thanks for coming to my flirting workshops, for going with me to the TV interviews, for always being so proud of me, and for flirting with me day in and day out. Thank you from the bottom of my heart for always being there to read and reread every word I wrote. Your input and willingness to help me while I was writing the manuscript is something I will always treasure. Thanks for putting our life on hold, for looking at the back of my head at the computer all day and all night, and for listening to all those, "So how does this sound?" Most of all, thanks for being "Exhibit A," for believing in me, and for always telling me that I could do it. You are and always will be the love of my life!

My gratitude goes to my incredible and caring editor, Amanda Waddell. Amanda, I feel that this is "our book." Thank you so much for making my words come alive. You helped me in so many ways. You were so encouraging and always knew how to boost my confidence and give me a pep talk when I so desperately needed it. I am truly grateful for everything you have done to make the book the best it could be. You are very gifted at your craft, and I am so lucky that you came into my life.

I am so fortunate to have Rosalind Wanke as my creative director. Your eye for detail, your flair for design, and your commitment to making the photos enhance my words was a phenomenal accomplishment. But most of all, thanks for the fabulous time we had in NYC for the photo shoot. Your friendship and professionalism will be cherished! You made a tedious task so much fun.

A huge thanks to Liudi Hara and his photographic team, for capturing all the flirting moves we possibly could and for all your painstaking efforts to make each photograph a perfect one.

And to the entire team at Fair Winds Press, especially design manager Meg Sniegoski and assistant managing editor Jen Grady—thank you for all of your help.

To my incredible family for always being so supportive and so proud of me, a very special thank you. I love you all.

Thank you to my wonderful friends, who always had the time to listen to parts of the manuscript, and who were always there for me: Roz, the 2 Carols, Gail, and Maryann.

Thank you to all my friends who have always shown sincere interest in my flirting accomplishments and endeavors. It has meant the world to me.

Thank you to Trish McDermott, formerly of Match.com, for hiring me and for always telling me I had to write a book. You have always been an inspiration to me and I thank you for everything you have done to get me on the bookshelves!

A warm and heartfelt thanks to all of you who have invited me to share my flirting knowledge: the Learning Annex, Princess Cruises, the New York Association for Psychiatric Rehabilitation, the Clubhouse of Suffolk, the Town of Brookhaven Women's Services, Columbia University, and so many more.

And finally, my biggest thank you goes to all of my participants and clients. Each of you has inspired me to write this book. Your personal struggles and triumphs have added so much to what I do. Thanks for sharing your flirting stories with me. It is because of you that I have been able to write this book. You are all my heroes!

ABOUT THE AUTHOR

Fran Greene, L.C.S.W., is a nationally renowned relationship expert and the former director of flirting at Match.com. She has appeared on the dating show *Wingman*, *Dateline NBC*, the *Today Show*, the *Travel Channel*, and more, and has been featured in the *New York Times*, the *Wall Street Journal*, *Cosmopolitan*, *Self*, *French Elle*, *Style*, *Good Housekeeping*, and *In Touch Weekly*.

   Fran runs a private practice in the New York City area working with singles who want to maximize their social lives and couples who want to improve their relationships. Through her ever-popular flirting workshops and seminars, she has helped thousands of people find love. To find out more, visit www.frangreene.com/.